IN HIS FOOTSTEPS

(A 52 Week Devotional)

Margaret J Makinde

IN HIS FOOTSTEPS

(A 52 Week Devotional)

Copyright © 2007 by Margaret J. Makinde
Revised in 2010
Printed in the United States of America
All rights reserved

ISBN 978-0-9840520-7-3

No part of this book may be reproduced or transmitted in any form by any means electronic or mechanical, including photocopying, recording by any information storage and retrieval system without prior written permission from the publisher.

All Scripture quotations except otherwise stated are from the King James Version of the Bible

PUBLISHED BY

T he Glad Tidings Inc
P.O. Box 334 Cumming, GA 30041
770-889-6261; www.thegladtidings.org

DEDICATED

To all who desire to follow, and walk in the Footsteps of Our Lord and Savior Jesus Christ

ACKNOWLEDGMENT

I am thankful to God for the grace to write this piece which I believe will greatly benefit Believers as they walk with God through the year. I am grateful and indebted to countless number of people who over the years have been instrumental to my achievements.

Specifically my thanks to the following people who through God's grace have helped me to advance in my walk with God – I am thankful to Nike and Remy Lawal, Ola and Sam Shitta-Bey. They contributed in various ways and at different times, in the activities of Christ Our Rock Ministries in reaching others with the Gospel.

My thanks and gratitude to my sister Mabel Oluboyede and to my sister in the LORD, Foluke Ogundiya who in unique ways helped in making my dreams come through. To my other brothers and sisters Professor Yomi Dinakin, Pastor Ope Dinakin, Nike Olowolabi, and Pastor Femi Dinakin, I am also grateful. I thank God for my sister Yinka who went to be with the LORD in December 2002.

I acknowledge these wonderful children who by their love and prayers encourage me in my walk with God. These are Lanre, Tobi, Tosin, Kemi, Layomi and Pelumi. I am thankful for Dara Makinde and Timi Makinde too.

Their lives have impacted and blessed mine. By reading this now, you can be sure they have prayed for you! Of course there are countless others whom God over the years have used to affect my life in one way or the other. My desire and prayer is that the Holy Spirit will reveal the Father's will to you through His Son Jesus Christ; that His Word will be a light to your path and a lamp to your feet – Psalm 119: 105.

Margaret J Makinde

PREFACE

In 2002, I was pasturing a new church. As a young man, I was full of energy and very busy with ministry. Similarly, the church conducted several programs and conferences and had a promising future. After praying and seeking God's face, and in response to His leading there was a change of course, and I followed Jesus' Footsteps to different area of ministry; to Homeless Shelters..

In His Footsteps is a devotional book that is a good Bible study companion for every Believer. It is a simple but powerful guide that ensures that the Believer consistently walks In Christ's Footsteps.

Pastor Margaret Makinde, I believe, has patiently and diligently listened to the voice of God while writing this awesome book. It has been of prime importance and I believe that piece receives the approval of Heaven.

Her experience in the Vineyard, coupled with her sound understanding of God's word, because of God's grace on her life has adequately equipped her for this divine assignment. **In His Footsteps** combines simplicity and power.

Thus, the Believer is strengthened. As you read this devotional book, it will become very evident that the Anointing of the Word rests upon this book. My prayer is that Christ's footprints will become clearer to you.

Pastor Samuel Jonathan.

CONTENTS

DEDICATION.. 3

ACKNOWLEDGMENT 4

PREFACE 5

CONTENTS...6

INTRODUCTION...8
THE BIBLE IN ONE YEAR 9

WEEKS 1-13...11

JOSEPH – A TYPE F JESUS 49

WEEKS 14-26..50

JOSHUA – A TYPE OF JESUS 89

WEEKS 27-39...94

JESUS IN ALL HUMAN ENDEAVORS.............134

WEEKS 40-52..136

IN CONCLUSION..179
HOW TO BECME A CHRISTIAN......................180

REFERENCES...183

INTRODUCTION

God spoke to mankind through His Word, and went further to speak to us in His Son, Jesus Christ our Savior, Redeemer and High Priest.

He still speaks to us today through the pages of the Bible, by the Holy Spirit through various channels including men and women, angels and other creatures as He pleases. In order to prosper in life we need to know the following:
- Trust God's Word which is the eternal Truth
- See the eternal truth in it; the Bible says you shall know the truth and the truth shall set you free.
- Know the Author – for holy men of God wrote as they were inspired by the Holy Spirit.
- See the background of the activities and words spoken by Bible characters. See the large picture, so that Scripture is not taken out of content.
- Seek and value expert as often as needed – for no Scripture is of any private interpretation.
- Live by and through the Word, for God is more interested in our character than our charisma!
- The only or first Bible that many will ever read is you. Therefore let your light shine before men that they may see your good work and glorify your Father Each Believer's life is expected to reflect the of God.

IN HIS FOOTSTEPS is prepared to be used as a weekly devotional to help in going through the Bible and to encourage all to walk with the Master and His wonderful Footsteps – 1 Peter 2: 17-18

THE BIBLE IN ONE YEAR

The Word of God according to Paul in 1 Corinthians 10: 11; and 2 Timothy 3: 16-17; is written for: -
- Our Instruction
- Our Admonition
- Our Correction and Reproof
- Our Profit
- Our Inspiration
- Propelling us to good works, knowing that we can touch God by faith; which comes by hearing (including reading, studying and pondering over), the Word of God.

Therefore it is pertinent for believers who truly want to walk with God to be armed with the Word of God. Once we seek Him in the volume/pages of His Book, with open hearts and a willingness to listen tithe Holy Spirit will reveal God to us through Jesus Christ.

> 1 Corinthians 10: 11 *Now all these things happened unto them for ensamples: and they are written for our admonition, upon whom the ends of the world are come*
>
> 2 Timothy 3: 16-17
> *16 All scripture is given by inspiration of God, and is profitable for doctrine, for reproof, for correction, for instruction in righteousness:*
> *17 That the man of God may be perfect, thoroughly furnished unto all good works.*

We must follow the rules for entering into the meaning and the spirit of the Word by reading:
- Continuously;
- Repeatedly;
- Independently;

- Prayerfully.
- Expecting to hear God speak through its pages

There are many reading plans available, but this will help us read through in a calendar year. The reader can choose to read through in one, two or more years, or follow different guidelines. The most important thing is to studiously read through and apply it, for it was given to us by God and He expects us to use it.

Below is plan to read through the Bible in one year from Genesis to Revelation, with no surprises.

Weekly Reading Plan

WEEK	BIBLE PASSAGE	WEEK	BIBLE PASSAGE
1	Genesis 1-25	27	Ecclesiastes; Song of Solomon
2	Genesis 26-50	28	Isaiah 1-24
3	Genesis 51-Exodus 19	29	Isaiah 25-48
4	Exodus 20-50	30	Isaiah 49-66; Song of Solomon
5	Leviticus 1-26	31	Jeremiah 1-24
6	Leviticus 27-Numbers 25	32	Jeremiah 25-46-52
7	Numbers 26-Deut.	33	Lamentations; Ezekiel 17
8	Leviticus -226	34	Ezekiel 18-35
9	Judges 1-25	35	Ezekiel 36-Daniel 9
10	Numbers 26-Deut.	36	Daniel 10-Hosea; Amos
11	1 Samuel 1-26-2 Samuel 20	37	Amos; Hosea; Obadiah
12	2 Samuel 21-1 Kings 17	38	Jonah; Micah; Nahum
13	1 Kings 18-2 Kings 20	39	Habakkuk; Zephaniah; Haggai
14	2 Kings 21-1 Chronicles 20	40	Zephaniah; Haggai; Zechariah; Malachi
15	2 Chronicles 21-1 Chronicles	41	Matthew 1-20; Nahum
16	2 Chronicles 21 Kings 20	42	Matthew 21; Haggai 11
17	2 Kings 21-1 Chronicles 20	43	Zephaniah; Zechariah; Malachi
18	1 Chronicles 21-2 Chronicles	44	Matthew 27-John 10
19	2 Chronicles 6-Ezra 10	45	John 11-Acts Mark 11
20	Nehemiah-Esther 10	46	Mark 12-17 Luke 16
21	Psalm 26-56	47	Romans 1 Corinthians 10
22	Psalm 57-82 50	48	1 Corinthians 1-2 Corinthians 13
23	Psalm 83-109	49	Ephesians; Galatians; 1, 2 Thess
24	Psalm 110-Proverbs 9	50	1 Timothy; Titus; Philemon
25	Psalm 57-82 21	51	Hebrews; James; 1, 2 Peter
26	Psalm 83-109		1 Ephesians; Revelation; 1, 2 Thess
24	Psalm 120-Proverbs 9		
25	Proverbs 10-21	50	1, 2 Timothy; Titus; Philemon
26	Proverbs 10-30	51	Hebrews; James; 1, 2 Peter

WEEKS 1-13

WEEK 1

THE LORD HE IS MY SHEPHERD...

Bible Passages: Psalm 1; 23; 121; John 10; Isaiah

Psalm 23: 1-2
1 The LORD is my shepherd; I shall not want...

Jesus confirming what the Psalmist wrote centuries before He physically came to earth makes us to know that He is the Good Shepherd. He knows His sheep and they know His voice and respond to the sound of His voice.

As the Good Shepherd, He cares for us individually, and goes after us to bring us to the fold when we go astray. Each one is unique and important, for with Him there is no respecter of persons. He goes after and takes care of each one of us even when we are in the midst of a very large crowd, when we appear to be irrelevant to others around us.

To Him we are not just a number, but each one fearfully and wonderfully made in the image of God. Therefore our word to all today is to run to Him, for shelter, protection and leading as we go through the labyrinth of life. There are times when the roads are dark or crooked; and the visions dim or blurred.

However we must recognize and acknowledge our Savior, Brother, Master and Mentor, the One who can lead us beside the still waters restore our souls and provide our every need.

His provision does not end today, because He makes our cup to run over, as He sets a table before us even in the midst of our enemies. His blessings are not kept until all our enemies are dead, because He does not want anyone to perish but that all will come to repentance.

Note also that as He blesses us our lives become testimonies of His goodness and mercy. It follows therefore that receiving from God is affected by how we relate to Him. He has given us His Word and His will; we are to key/fit into His plan for us by allowing Him to be Lord of our lives. Therefore relax in Him and be sure that He who watches over you - the God of Israel, does not slumber nor sleep – Psalm 121:4.

... I Shall Not Want

- *The Lord He is my Shepherd* – RELATIONSHIP with God!
- *I shall not want* – SUPPLY from the Jehovah Jireh!
- *He maketh me to lie down in green pastures* – REST, at His right hand there are pleasures forever!
- *He leadeth me beside still waters* – REFRESHMENT because I wait in Him so I run I am not tired and walk and not weary!
- *He restoreth my soul* – HEALING; He is the balm of Gilead!
- *He leadeth me in the paths of righteousness* – GUIDANCE; He leads me by His spirit into all truth for He is truth!
- *For His name sake* – REPOSE, I am called by His name!

- *Yea, though I walk through the valley of the shadow of death* – TESTING; He does not tempt beyond the grace He gave!
- *I will fear no evil* – PROTECTION from seen and unseen enemies, at all times and in all situations!
- *For thou art with me* – FAITHFULNESS; even when I am not faithful, He will is
- *Thy rod and thy staff they comfort me* – THAT'S DISCIPLINE; He chastises those He loves!
- *Thou preparest a table before me in the presence of mine enemies* – HOPE; let not my adversaries rejoice over me when I fall, my hope in Him is sure
- *Thou anointest my head with oil* – THAT IS CONSECRATION! – I am consecrated by Him and for Him
- *My cup runneth over* – THAT IS ABUNDANCE; even in the midst of famine! Jesus said that there is no lack in His and our Father's house
- *Surely goodness and mercy shall follow me all the days of my life* – BLESSED to be a blessing!
- *And I will dwell in the house of the Lord forever* – ETERNAL SECURITY!

Who is your shepherd? Christ Jesus our Chief Shepherd is able to keep all that turn to Him for protection and guidance. He is waiting to receive you into the fold which is ever growing!

Prayer Points:

Dear LORD, help me to see God in everything that I do, with assurance that the LORD is with at all times

WEEK 2

JESUS CHRIST: He that Abides in Him... ...

Bible Passages: John 15; 1 Corinthians2; Philippians 3

> John 15: 4-11
> 4 Abide in me, and I in you. As the branch cannot bear fruit of itself, except it abide in the vine; no more can ye, except ye abide in me
> 5 I am the vine, ye are the branches: He that abideth in me, and I in him, the same bringeth forth much fruit: for without me ye can do nothing.
> 6 If a man abide not in me, he is cast forth as a branch, and is withered; and men gather them, and cast them into the fire, and they are burned...

Some of the ways by which we know that an object is alive are: Growth; Reproduction; and Fruitfulness. When God created man, it was for specific plans and purposes. We always have to go back to the beginning of creation in order to appreciate where we are in Christ according to God's standards.

Whether we make it or not depends on if we fulfill His plans for creating us (Genesis Chapter two); primarily to SUBDUE THE EARTH – through procreation and replenishment. We must also consider our successes in line with His specific plans for us as individuals.

God purposed and commanded that we have dominion, be fruitful and multiply, not just bringing forth one or two, but MULTIPLYING! This has not always been the case, in the lives of people, including Christians all through human history.

One thing about God is that His demands from us, in order to live victorious lives are simple and appear foolish to the carnal mind. He is Spirit and beyond human comprehension!

His creatures do not only have to follow His divine plan for things to work right, they have to wait on His timing, and the order He purposed things to operate. He is kind, loving, merciful, just, and does not change – both in character and splendor. Briefly therefore let us touch on one key that Jesus gave us in order to prosper – ABIDING IN HIM – John. 15: 4-10.

That way we can draw strength from Him, grow, and bear fruit like Him and as God purposed for us. Abiding in Him involves being grafted to, sticking to thereby depending on Him for all the resources necessary for life and fulfillment of our destinies. We must stick to Him, so much so that we look like Him and reflect His character, no matter the situation or circumstance may be saying.

Once we are truly grafted to Him, then He is our Source and we can then say, like Paul affirmed to the Ephesians in Acts 17:28 in *Him we live and move and have our being*. He lives through us; hence we can say that the lives that we live are His! He demands complete obedience from us, and we must understand that with God partial obedience is disobedience.

Jesus Christ our Prime Example and Chief Apostle demonstrated to us that it is possible to obey God at all times by His life on earth and death on the cross at Calvary. He kept His focus on God His and our Father; He achieved all that by abiding (submitting His will to) that of our Father to redeem us.

This One Thing I Do...

Yesterday is gone; it is now a part of history, never to see the light of day again. Today is new; with all the opportunities, possibilities, challenges, successes and failures that our actions, choices, reactions, and attitudes keep unfolding as the time that waits for no man keeps ticking on.

Tomorrow is intact in God's hands, fresh with great and unimaginable opportunities for each and every one of God's creatures. In order to enter into the fullness of what God has prepared for our future both immediate and the long term, we must be ready to: -

- Learn to apply the knowledge we acquire from the past to help us make the right decisions to be able to make the best use of today.

- Learn not to relish on past successes and failures, because the best the past can do for us is to give us experience. We know that experience cannot take us to our destiny, but the Word of God can.

- Keep our focus on God and the hope of His eternal destiny for those who love Him, assured that whatever we are facing is to work for our good.

We are called to redeem the time not to relieve it! So what have been doing with every new day that God blesses you with! Each new day is gift from God, packaged with new mercies and hope; and hope does not make one ashamed!

Prayer Point:

To abide and keep my focus on the Good Shepherd

WEEK 3

IT SHALL COME TO PASS

Bible Passages: Zechariah 8; Isaiah 14: 3; Psalm 91; Corinthians 10; 1Peter 1

Zechariah 8: 13 *And it shall come to pass that as ye were a curse among the heathen, O house of Judah, and house of Israel; so will I save you and ye shall be a blessing, fear not, but let your hands be strong.*

Isaiah 14: 3-5
*3 And it shall come to pass in the day that the LORD shall give thee rest from thy sorrow, and from thy fear, and from the hard bondage wherein thou wast made to serve...*It does not matter the situation you find yourself in today note that - IT SHALL COME TO PASS! Why! –

This is because it has a beginning! Jesus makes us to know that heaven and earth shall pass away but that neither a jot, nor a dot will pass away from the Word of God. The assurance we have as believers is that, whether we are alive here on earth or there with Him in heaven, whether in sickness or health, in favorable or unfavorable situations and circumstances the Kingdom of God is our portion. His love for our lives and us is real and ever new.

Let us therefore, hold on to the real issues of life in His word that makes us to know that - 1 Corinthians 2: 9. *DO YOU LOVE GOD?* His Word abides forever. His Word does not change therefore we can be sure that if we love Him, there is a bright light at the end of this seemingly endless tunnel. The tunnel has a beginning; therefore it must have an end.

For everything that has a beginning must of necessity have an end. In other words, the tunnel, and the one passing through it will soon become history just like the one who dug it - be it the devil, a spirit, or man – whoever it is, shall soon come to pass.

With this assurance we should come to terms with God's gift of His peace that passes all understanding. His peace empowers us to live above all the challenges and obstacles the enemy put along our way, as we journey through life. Note that it does not matter how great, massive or persistent they may be; they *shall surely come to pass.*

This is because the devil that puts the obstacle there has a beginning, likewise the obstacles he puts; and everything that has a beginning must of necessity have an end. The Only One who is endless is our God who reigns eternally, and His word assures us that we are more than conquerors.

So a responsibility is placed on us to keep our focus on Him who can change our situations and circumstance and whose love and grace do not diminish nor wane. His ability to save and deliver is the same yesterday, today and will always be. But our situations are subject to changing seasons, places and positions; acquaintances and factors too numerous to list.

But whatever the situation *it shall soon come to pass,* just like the person experiencing it! Have you ever given this statement a thought before? If not, please do so today, because everything that has a beginning must of necessity have an end. It therefore, implies that, whatever situation or circumstance you may find yourself in today – *It shall come to pass!* That situation will soon become history just like the person going through it, whether you believe it or not.

No matter how long we live *all flesh is as grass and the glory of man like the flower thereof* – 1Peter 1: 24. Therefore why fret, when these shall soon come to pass. It is time for Believers to come to terms with this fact – that is the transient nature of man and all that pertain to him. If man's life is so fleeting, how then do we fret over the activities within such a temporary part of our existence?

Relax; take charge as you are supposed to. God gave us dominion over all other creatures, as well authority over our lives. Therefore we need to take control of our emotions, and thoughts

The Book of Ecclesiastes tells us that the life of man including, and inclusive of its sorrows, successes, failures and achievements is "vanity upon vanity", and not worth all the attention that man over the ages have put into it.

This is achievable if we dwell in His secret place, thereby being privileged to know His mind for us even when we are confronted with issues that are not favorable to us. We shall abide under the shadow of the Almighty – Psalm 91.

Prayer Points:

Dear LORD, please help me to be able to stand against the aggression of the devil.

WEEK 4
IT SHALL SURELY COME TO PASS

Bible Passages: Hosea 2; Malachi 3, Philippians 4; Matthew 24; Mark 13

Mark 13: 31 *Heaven and earth shall pass away: but my words shall not pass away.*

Matthew 24: 35 *Heaven and earth shall pass away, but my words shall not pass away...*

We continue to ponder over the statement - *"It shall come to pass."* Have you ever considered the fact that; whatsoever the situation you find yourself in today *that - IT SHALL COME TO PASS! Why! - This is because it has a beginning!*

Jesus makes us to know that heaven and earth shall pass away but that neither a jot, nor a dot will pass away from the Word of God. The assurance we have as believers is that, no matter the situations and circumstances we find ourselves the Kingdom of God is our portion. His love for our lives and us is real and new as ever.

Let us therefore, hold on to the real issues of life in His word. Apostle James says we should allow the things we are going through to perfect, rather than break us – James 1: 2-5. There is much to be accomplished for our Father. We must not allow the enemy to make us keep our focus on situations and circumstances of life which like us will soon pass away.

Let us focus on God who is able to do all things. He is also the Restorer of broken vessels. There is one great assurance that we have in Christ Jesus, who has given us the victory. No matter how tough the situation is, or gets, just hold on, and have faith in Him.

We are not supposed to move by faith and not by sight, nor feelings, no matter how hopeless the situation may be. After all the Joy of the LORD is our strength.

Allow your faith to move the mountain and not vice versa! Victory is yours for the taking – Pick it up! Consider "Faith and Fear" as they affect us today to determine what comes up in the future of our lives here and there.

It is only through faith in God and His Word that we can subdue kingdoms, pull down strongholds, and stop the mouth of lions, turn to flight the armies ... Hebrews 11: 29-35. Success and victory await us as we face the challenges of today, boldly, and courageously, relying on God through His Word and His Spirit to perfect all that concerns us. Like Caleb we are well able, as we hold on to God's precious promises.

Faith is the victory! It is stronger than death, and cannot be stopped! We have established through the Word of God that heaven and earth shall pass away, but that His Word abides forever. So it does not matter whether in old or new earth/heaven, the word of God is the same and eternally true.

Situations and circumstances cannot change the Word of God, rather the Word changes lives, nations, situations and circumstances at God's instance. This has been the case in all ages and will be forever.

Armed with this truth, we know that in years to come just like our forefathers we will cease to exist here on earth. Methuselah, the man recorded to have lived for 969 years – Genesis 5: 27; is no still got expended and died like all mortals

So no matter the issues whether successes, failures, in abundance or lack that we face or are confronted with they will be no more as soon as the one facing them leaves the scene –

The world is after all is a stage where each person is an actor prepared for different parts and functions! So all our experiences will soon *come to pass!* As we go through life, we expect that changes will take place for our good as we rely on the word of God, irrespective of what we are experiencing at the present.

Being adequately armed with His word we can change situations through Him who does not change. Note that we must desire and ask for change by faith and trust God to make the change through Christ Jesus, by the Holy Spirit – Philippians 4: 13 *I can do all things through Christ which strengtheneth me.*

Malachi 3: 6 *For I am the Lord, I do not change; Therefore you are not consumed, O sons of Jacob.* God does not change and His mercies are new every day, so we are sure of His constant readiness to be able to meet our every need. We must therefore be prepared to take the necessary steps towards getting the required changes.

Prayer Points:

Dear LORD, please replace my fear with faith in Christ Jesus.

WEEK 5

OUR GOD IS...
I. A God of Purpose;
II. A God of Plan;
III. A God of Order

Bible Passages: Genesis 18; Isaiah 60; Jeremiah 29; Daniel 2; Matthew 5: 36; 11: 27; 1 Corinthians 2: 9; Luke 4; Revelation 1

1 Corinthians 2: 9 *But as it is written, Eye hath not seen, nor ear heard, neither have entered into the heart of man, the things which God hath prepared for them that love him.*

I. A God of Purpose: In all the activities of God that we see, there is an ultimate purpose for which He does everything. For instance we see and hear Him give reason all the things He created, even in setting boundaries for day and night, the sun the moon and the stars; the seas and the dry land all had specific function for being put into being.

Ultimately it is to glorify God. And all have seasons and times for which they are to manifest the glory of God. Most importantly His plans never change because He does not. He created the woman to be a helpmeet for the woman, each with defined roles and responsibilities, to each other and to God.

He gave us free will; that is creating us in His own image. Thus we are supposed to have dominion over all the creatures that inhabit the earth including Satan that was thrown down from heaven, before we ever came to the scene.

II. A God of Plan

Before God created man (male and female – Adam and Eve), and put him in the Garden of Eden,

He knew man would fall to the temptation of Satan; thereby lose his high estate. So He already made a plan for redemption, even before man came to the scene. This is because He is All-knowing as well as Almighty. God cannot be taken by surprise, He is Alpha and Omega, and He knows the end from the beginning, hence the Reconciliation of man to God, was planned in heaven, long before man was created.

It follows therefore that since we cannot make a strand of our hair black or gray – Matthew 5: 36, we must turn to the Master Planner for direction in order to fulfill destiny! He has destined us for greatness and knew about all the stumbling blocks along our ways and therefore prepared a way of escape for each and every one of them. Only we must call and depend on Him at all times, showing that we depend on Him

III. A God of Order

Luke 4: 21 *And he began to say unto them, This day is this scripture fulfilled in your ears.* God works even when there is chaos; the first thing He does is to put order into the situation that is chaotic

He is a Great Architect, and an Awesome Organizer, who is very interested in every detail and every arrangement of each and every creature that He made. Moreover our God has a perfect sense of beauty, coordination and organization. For as long as the earth remains there will be a seed time and a harvest time, irrespective of which generation we are in.

Each generation of humanity has always sought food, shelter, knowledge and power. God's ways are always perfect and the same yesterday today and tomorrow.

It does not matter which generation you in. For instance in order to eat a fish it must go through
- Being caught and cleaned
- Cooked/Processed and eaten to be digested

He made Himself an Example; chose a crop of disciples from different walks of life and backgrounds, to show that He is after the heart and that no one is too poor to be raised and trained for the work of ministry! Willingness is the key to working in God's vineyard!

Are you ready to reign with Him; then join the bandwagon of the saints and take the Gospel to the nooks and corners of the earth – for the Gospel is the power of God to salvation to them that believe?
- He purposes to reconcile us with Him, but we must follow His order, by first accepting His Son Jesus the Messiah as Lord and Savior.
- He purposed for us to shine, even in the midst of the gross darkness that covers the earth – Isaiah 60: 1-2. Sin brings disorder and disorganization; when we come to the saving grace of God through His Son Jesus He rearranges, reorganizes sets our lives in order.
- He purposed that be kept in perfect peace if our minds are stayed on Him – Isaiah 26: 3.

- He purposed that we live in victory by having faith in Him – Habakkuk 2: 4; Romans 1: 17; Galatians 3: 11; Hebrews 10: 30; 1John 5: 4,

Prayer Points:

Dear LORD, please help me to know Your plans for my life and abide in Christ

WEEK 6

WHAT IS IN A NAME?

Bible Passages: Matthew 1-2; Psalm 139

Matthew 1: 23 *Behold, a virgin shall be with child, and shall bring forth a son, and they shall call his name Emmanuel, which being interpreted is, God with us.*

Let's take a look at how our name, positioning, and placement reflect our lives. Each person created by God is unique and purposed for a very unique assignment. However the earth is filled with so many things that tend to divert us from our destiny – consider the case of

- Abram, who was destined to be the father of nations, his name changed to Abraham to reflect this. His wife's name Sarai changed to Sarah, to reflect their unique position in the plan of God for humanity.
- Jacob which means Supplanter, who was destined to be a prince had to be change to Israel to reflect who he is really should be.

– Jabez who was named a son of sorrow, but who knew that God destined His children for greatness– 1 Chronicles 4: 9-10, so he requested for a change of status from the God of Israel who is able to make us fulfill destiny.

This is an indication of the fact that though our physical names may not be changed, but spiritually our destiny is set in the order that God purposed for it. God has given each person a will and an ability to choose to do what he/she is purposed for or otherwise.

The responsibilities on us: are:

1. To find God's purpose for our lives
2. How we stand in fulfilling this purpose
3. If we are short of fulfilling His plans and purposes, we are to ask Him to help us to make the necessary changes – whether in positioning, attitude, acquaintances, profession, and other things in order to be WHOM HE WANTS US TO BE.

Our names must reflect who we are in Christ Jesus. Does your name reflect God's workings in your life?

Who was Asaph?

Bible Passages: 2 Chronicles 15-16; 14; Psalm 73; Daniel 4

1 Chronicles 15: 16-19
16 And David spake to the chief of the Levites to appoint their brethren to be the singers with instruments of musick, psalteries and harps and cymbals, sounding, by lifting up the voice with joy.

17 So the Levites appointed Heman the son of Joel; and of his brethren, Asaph the son of Berechiah; and of the sons of Merari their brethren, Ethan the son of Kushaiah;
18 And with them their brethren of the second degree, Zechariah, Ben, and Jaaziel, and Shemiramoth, and Jehiel, and Unni, Eliab, and Benaiah, and Maaseiah, and Mattithiah, and Elipheleh, and Mikneiah, and Obededom, and Jeiel, the porters.
19 So the singers, Heman, Asaph, and Ethan, were appointed to sound with cymbals of brass;

Asaph which means *God has gathered* is the name of five Old Testament men.

But we want to consider the one who was the son of Berachiah a Gershonite, who sounded cymbals before the Ark of the Covenant, when it was moved from the house of Obed-Edom to Jerusalem – 1 Chronicles 16.

David put Asaph in charge of praising and thanking God. Several of David's Psalms have a subtitle – To the Director of Music. Twelve Psalms are attributed to the family of Asaph – Psalms 50; 73-83.

Let us consider Psalm 73 to see how Asaph found answers to the questions that we like him still ask God today. From this we know that the quality of the answers we get depends on where we turn to for answers – Psalm 73: 17 *until I went into the sanctuary of God; then understood I......*
- When he went into the Sanctuary of God which is a spiritual hiding place, he found new perspective and understanding of life. In God's presence everything changed except his circumstances.

- Until he entered the Sanctuary, Asaph was overwhelmed by the unfairness of present circumstances. In the Sanctuary, he saw how different those same inequalities would look on the day God holds court with His enemies!
- He had been focusing on the unfairness of life rather than on the One who would settle the score in a perfect and just way.
- God's work in the present can be trusted because He has perfect knowledge of the future. He concluded king Nebuchadnezzar – Daniel 4: 34-35. God is sovereign worthy of praise and acknowledgement and trust.

Prayer Points:

That I may consistently look up to, and wait on God, for answers to all my questions.

WEEK 7

KNOW YOUR ENEMY – He comes to steal...

Bible Passages: John 10: 10-11; Matthew 11; 13; Romans 14: 17; Philippians 3; Ephesians 3

John 10: 10
10 The thief cometh not, but for to steal, and to kill, and to destroy: I am come that they might have life, and that they might have it more abundantly.

Walking right with God involves knowing Him who redeemed and accepted us into the beloved through His Son Jesus our Messiah. Truly we chose to receive Him into our hearts, but we must realize that He first found and chose us. Moreover the enemy of God – the Devil who also our number one enemy does not want us to fulfill destiny and God's purposes and plans for our lives.

Having tried to prevent us to accept Jesus as Lord and savior of our lives, he is unrelenting in his effort to draw us away from Him. Jesus warns in John 10: 10 that, he *comes to steal, kill and destroy.* He is also waiting for an opportune time mostly when we are vulnerable to attack and challenge our choices and position in Christ Jesus.

All though the Scriptures we see that God wants us to know Him; His love power and will for humanity. God through the Scriptures, in the lives of the patriarchs, prophets and through the life of His Son reveals His nature and character to us.

The kingdom of God is not in meat and drink but in love power and joy in the Holy Ghost – Romans 14: 17.

It follows that if one of the ingredients of the kingdom of God is power; there must be a necessity to use the power given! In Matthew 11: 12 *And from the days of John the Baptist until now the kingdom of God suffereth violence, and the violent take it by force.*

We also notice that God desires that we know and understand the tactics of the devil, His and our enemy. It is in doing this that we can confidently live victorious lives that He has prepared for each and every one of us. God desires that we know the purpose and tactics of our enemy.

This is to help us in our preparedness to resist him and make our walk with God more pleasurable. For instance our knowledge of the fact that the enemy is not as ugly as he is being portrayed by artists and the pictures of him that we see, and that his suggestions do not always show the resultant pains that could come from following his ways.

This helps us to be able to look at things more closely and to let us know that only the Word of God is the standard by which all our decisions and actions must be based.

Know Your Enemy – He sows seeds of Evil

Matthew 13: 39-41
39 The enemy that sowed them is the devil; the harvest is the end of the world; and the reapers are the angels.
40 As therefore the tares are gathered and burned in the fire; so shall it be in the end of this world....
Let us continue the discussion on the responsibility of believers to find out the tricks and tactics of the Devil our enemy. For instance:

- Moses was brought up in Pharaoh's palace, knew the crafts of Egypt; demanded freedom for his people.
- Moses also sent twelve spies to the Promised Land, before they moved in to take possession of it.
- Esther became queen in the very palace of the king who had the Israelites enslaved in his kingdom.
- David was musician to Saul, the very king who wanted to kill him in order to prevent from inheriting the kingdom as ordained by God

From these and other experiences in the Bible we see:-

- God has prepared and purposed that we live in abundance, but He respects our views and responds to us the way we respond to Him and His Word. He will not impose victory on us! We are to PRESS towards the goal set before us – Philippians 3: 14; Ephesians 3: 20.

- The Devil is a liar and sows the seed of lies into the lives of as many as will give him audience. Where there is peace he sows the seed of disharmony, discord and confusion; where there love, bitterness, hatred, fear and disunity in order to disorganize and disorientate God's children.
- Our perception of the enemy is vital to our victory. Our victory is affected by our PERCEPTION of God, the devil and ourselves.

Prayer Points:

To be able to keep my focus on God and live in victory

WEEK 8

JESUS CHRIST –

The Author and Finisher of our Faith

Bible Passages: Hebrews 11: 31-40; 12; 1 John 5; Matthew 10; Romans 9; Philippians 2

Hebrews 12: 2 ...*Looking unto Jesus the author and the finisher of our faith that endureth to the end shall be saved.*

Paul compares the Christian to an athlete. Like in the Olympic Games, the contenders were often greatly animated by the consideration that the eyes of the principal men of their country were fixed upon them; so they make extraordinary exertions. The Greeks and Latin frequently use the term cloud, to express a great number of persons or things.

Just like those who run in the Olympic races would throw aside everything that might impede them in their course; so Christians, professing heaven as their ultimate destination, must throw aside everything that might hinder them in their Christian race.

We must recognize and deal with whatever weighs down our hearts or affections to earth. No man, with the love of the world in his heart, can ever reach the kingdom of heaven. – Matthew 6: 25. We must look away from the world and all secular concerns; put our gaze on Jesus and all the spiritual and heavenly things connected with Him.

In the Grecian games; those who ran were to keep their eyes fixed on the mark of the prize; keep the goal in view. This implies that we should: -
- Place all our hope and confidence in Christ, who is our sole Source of strength in this race of faith.
- Consider Him our Leader in this contest
- Consider Him the Captain; Leader – Hebrews 2: 10.

He also, Judges in the games; Admits the contenders, and Gives the prizes to the winners. Jesus is here represented as the officer, and every Christian a contender in this race of life. The heavenly race is begun and completed under the authority and supervision of Jesus.

He is the One under whom and by whose permission and direction, according to the rules of the heavenly race, we are permitted to enter, and commence the race. We can continue the race only for as long as we abide in Him and His will for our lives.

That way we have constant and continuous nourishment and energy to continue to run and advance. He is the Finisher, the One who perfects, by awarding and giving the prizes, to the participants at the end of the race. He declares the winners – these are the ones who endure to the end – Matthew 10: 22; Revelation 2: 26; 3: 5-21.

No one comes to the Father except through Christ. He it is who draws us to Him by the reason of His atoning blood, by His grace and mercy – Romans 9: 14-17; 5: 1-2.

Everyone is kept in the race only by His grace through His eternal Holy Spirit. Having endured the cross and despised the shame of this ignominious death for our sake, He is now set down at the right hand of God, ever appearing in the presence of God for us.

He continues His exhibition of Himself as our Sacrifice, and His intercession as our Mediator. Jesus endured the cross, not in the prospect of gaining an everlasting glory. He had the fullness of that glory with the Father before the – John 17-5.

Life is like a race, and each goal of our lives is like a race, for in each situation we aspire to reach certain destinations; which we set by the leading of God or through a revelation of His will for our lives. Recognizing that of our own we are without strength, why don't you ask Him for the faith to continue and finish the race of your life today?

Along the way there are hills, mountains, valleys and potholes that the enemy and his cohorts place on our path. He only gives in response to our asking. He gives liberally and does not reprimand you for being weak; He knows the level of your strength before you began the race and will give and perfect your faith in Him!

Knowing that we can only touch Him by faith we must humbly approach God through the Blood of the Lamb and with His word in our mouths. In conclusion Jesus begins our faith in regeneration and perfects our faith in sanctification. With a faith not only begun but also perfected, by Christ are we are able to run this race, keeping our eyes on Him.

Prayer Points:

Lord Jesus I need you every day of my life.

WEEK 9

THE GOSPEL OF JESUS CHRIST

Bible Passages: Romans 1; 10; Matthew 24: 14; Luke 24: 44-47; John 1:12; 3:16, 36; Acts 16; 28: 24

Romans 1: 16 *For I am not ashamed of the gospel, for it is God's power for salvation to everyone who believes, to the Jew first and also to the Greek* (NET).

Matthew 24: 14 *And this gospel of the kingdom shall be preached in the entire world for a witness unto all nations; and then shall the end come.*

God has a good word for us. His way of man's right standing with Him is revealed in this good news. In the New Testament it denotes the good tidings of the Kingdom of God and of salvation through Christ Jesus, which must be received by faith, on the basis of His expiatory death, His resurrection and ascension to heaven. The word "Gospel", means "Good News", occurs a number of times in the New Testament. It is described as The Gospel of: -
- God – Romans 1:1;
- Christ – Romans 1:16;
- The glory of Christ – 2 Corinthians 4:4;
- Your salvation – Ephesians 1:13;
- Peace – Ephesians 6:15;
- Or The everlasting gospel – Revelation 14:6.

The source of the gospel determines its character. The gospel is good news from God. The difference between the gospel of God and the religion of man is that man's religion begins with man, while God's gospel always begins with God.

The Good News is that God sent Jesus Christ, His only Son, into this world to die upon the cross and rise from the dead to save us from our sins.

Having done this, God has raised Him from the dead, and He is now a living Savior exalted at His right hand – Hebrews 7:25-26. The Gospel message is the declaration of the glorious Person of Christ, of His Finished Work and of His present saving power, to save sinful man. The gospel is the instrument of God's power that brings salvation to all who believe in it.

Man's primary need is salvation, and the gospel is God's manifest power to save sinners. The gospel is for everyone for Jew and Gentile alike. Salvation is simple; all that is needed is to believe the GOOD NEWS!

Do you believe?

Read John 1:12; John 3:16; John 3:36; Acts 16:30-31;

Romans 10:9-10; Acts 28:24

The Wise Ones Took Oil In Their Vessels

Bible Passages: Matthew 25; Ecclesiastes 8 Daniel 2; Proverbs 4

Matthew 25: 4 But *the wise took oil in their vessels with their lamps.*

Ecclesiastes 8: 1 *Who is as the wise man? and who knoweth the interpretation of a thing? a man's wisdom maketh his face to shine, and the boldness of his face shall be changed.*

Jesus told two parables about wise – one on the wise man who built his house on the rock Matthew 7: 24-28, and these maidens who took oil their lamps. From Proverbs 4: 7, we know that we are involved in the issue of our wisdom in life!

The decision to be wise, just like that of being saved is ours; the power to save is in the Word, through the Holy Spirit. God expects us to be wise, by being prepared for the second coming of the Messiah. Assuredly, He will come again – Acts 1: 11.

Though no one knows when, but we must be ready. Notice the common factors in these ten virgins: -

- They were all virgins
- They all had lamps and oil to start with. They all slept – Each is subject to sin, tiredness and failure.

The only difference between them was that the wise had enough oil for their lamps, while the foolish ones burnt theirs out! Do you have enough oil in your lamp? It is not just to have oil; there must be enough oil, for our Bridegroom comes for only those who are eagerly awaiting His return.

He that endures to the end shall be saved. It is not enough to wake up; there must be oil for the lamp when we the trumpet sounds. He may come now, so watch and pray, as Jesus commanded in Matthew 24:13; 42. Jesus is coming back gloriously, for His Bride – the Church that includes you!

The same power that raised Jesus from the dead is still available to keep us alive! So be wise, for His return is imminent! Are you prepared for Him?

Prayer Points:
Dear LORD, give me strength to watch and pray, and be ready for my Lord's and King's soon return

WEEK 10

ARE YOU PRAYING GOD'S WAY?

Bible Passages: Proverbs 14: *34;* Hebrews *12: 14;* Psalm 24: 3-5; Psalms 1 and 92

1 Peter 3:12 *For the eyes of the Lord are over the righteous, and his ears are open unto their prayers: but the face of the Lord is against them that do evil.*

Prayer is necessary and the important in the lives of people and especially Believers. Every one prays, but God demands that we pray to Him, constantly and consistently. That we be in His presence at all times. Prayer shows and molds our character. The more time we spend in God's presence, the more we:
- Reveal His glory
- Manifest His power; and
- Reflect His Light

Prayer is the means by which lesser beings communicate with a more superior one in order to receive his blessings.
- WHY DO WE PRAY?
- WHEN DO WE PRAY?
- HOW DO WE PRAY?
- WHERE DO WE PRAY?
- TO WHOM DO WE PRAY?

For Christians and Believers, prayer/praying, is the vehicle with which we reach and relate with our Father.

In order to pray effectively we must understand the prerequisite for praying.
- God's Word abides for ever; it is eternal and unchanging
- God is Spirit and all who must worship (a form of communication) Him must do so in spirit and in truth –
- God's thoughts towards us are thoughts of peace – Jeremiah 29: 11
- He desires that we be in health , spirit soul and body– 3 John 2

- He says He will not deny us the desires of our hearts, or the requests of our lips – Psalm 21: 2 *Thou hast given him his heart's desire, and hast not withholden the request of his lips. Selah.*

God demands that we walk by faith, holy, righteous and blameless before Him –in the place of prayers:
- 1 Peter 3:12
- Proverbs 14: *34*
- Hebrews *12: 14*
- Psalm 24: 3-5;
- Psalms 1 and 92

Pray Without Ceasing!

Bible Passages: Luke 18: 1-8; Hebrews 11; *12:;* Psalm 24: 3-5; Psalms 1 and 92

Luke 18: 1-8
1 And he spake a parable unto them to this end, that men ought always to pray, and not to faint;
2 Saying, There was in a city a judge, which feared not God, neither regarded man:
3 And there was a widow in that city; and she came unto him, saying, Avenge me of mine adversary.

God demands that we do not relent in calling on Him consistently and persistently until we receive answers to our prayers.

We must be aware that every area is covered; that is like this widow, who was sure she will be vindicated, and like David who affirmed that there must be no iniquity in his heart for God to answer him – Psalm 66: 18 *If I regard iniquity in my heart, the Lord will not hear me*

We must realize too that our coming to the presence of the LORD in prayers must not always be to petition for our needs. Rather we must be willing to go to Him to tell Him how much we;

- Love and Appreciate Him for He is and what He had done for us;
- Praise and worship Him because He demands that and He created us for His praise;
- Praise Him in anticipation of what He will yet do for He has great plans for our future - 1 Corinthians 2:9; and thereby we manifest our faith and trust in Him.

Prayer Points:
To praise God continually and to reap a harvest of joy and abundance

WEEK 11

THE GENERAL EPISTLES

Bible Passages: Romans 15: 4; 1 Corinthians 10; Luke 1

Romans 15: 4 *For whatsoever things were written aforetime were written for our learning, that we through patience and comfort of the scriptures might have hope.*

- Hebrews portrays Christ as the better way of salvation: better than anything that Old Testament Judaism could provide. He is the ONLY way that leads to God and freedom from sin that leads to death and destruction.
- James integrates true faith and everyday experience by stressing that genuine faith that genuine faith works, that faith must be backed up with action. That is true faith is seen is demonstrated by action.
- Peter's Epistles are manuals on how to handle suffering from within and without. Suffering is still around for as long as we are in the world, but as believers we are to learn to live above it as we look to Jesus our Example.
- John's letters encourage fellowship with God and other believers for victorious Christian living.
- Jude sounds the battles cry to defend the Gospel
- Revelation encourages faithful believers of all ages to stand firm in the midst of persecution.

Believers must await the return of Christ in power and glory as promised all through the Scriptures. More importantly however as believers we are to be prepared and watch for the coming of the LORD, who is Christ Jesus. He said in Luke 12: 34-40 ... *40*

No one knows when He will come again, but we are sure He will and we know how He will – the same way He went away – in the clouds; all eyes shall be able to see Him. Unlike the first time when He came quietly and humbly, this time He is coming with power and in glory. Moreover unlike the first time when He came and mingled with

The Call to Discipleship

Bible Passages: Matthew 16:24; Mark 2: 14; 4: 19; Luke 9: 57-62

Jesus came to establish the Kingdom of God here on earth. This is Kingdom different from man's understanding of what a kingdom is supposed to be. This is a Kingdom of love power, and joy in the Holy Ghost – Romans 14: 17. To do this He started with a crop of disciples and to perpetuate it the call to discipleship is on for as long as the earth remains.

The call to discipleship is on Christ's terms, not ours, and the cost determined by the Lord, and not by the disciples. At the end of His ministry, the day of His crucifixion, Jesus owned nothing, but the clothes on His back.

The cost of discipleship for Jesus was high. It cost Him His life in execution as a criminal to follow the will of His heavenly Father. Jesus was obedient unto death. Jesus calls us to radical discipleship. This might be the reason so many drop out after joining up

Jesus' call to discipleship is radical – *Allow the dead to bury their own dead; but as for you, go and proclaim everywhere the Kingdom of God* – Luke 9: 60.

Let the spiritual dead bury the dead. They are dead to spiritual realities. On the other hand, those who are spiritually alive will drop everything, counting the cost, to follow Jesus as Lord. Discipleship:

- demands that we drop everything, even our families. That is anyone who would seek to exercise a higher relationship of affection in our lives? Consider the lives of Elisha and Elijah in the Old Testament; Matthew the Levite, Peter James and John and Paul who completely changed course in the New Testament.
- Makes us chose between Christ and others.

What really matters is our submission to the will of God (OBEDIENCE). The disciple of Jesus Christ cannot live to please himself but God through Christ. He can live only to please the King. Are you a true disciple?

<u>Prayer Points</u>:

1. To follow Christ more closely, and surrender my heart to the LORD

WEEK 12

THREE WONDERFUL THINGS TO CONSIDER!

 Bible Passages: Proverbs 30: 18-19

Proverbs 30: 18-19
18 There be three things which are too wonderful for me, yea, four which I know not:

Just as the:
- Serpent must rely on instinct to know his destination as he passes on the rock. No one can trace his path to and from his shelter in the rocks; it finds its way back and forth!
- The eagle flies to and fro in the sky, looking for prey and takes food to its offspring in a secure place on the mountains, with no compass; it finds it way by relying on its God given instinct and sense of direction. There are no roads in the sky, yet the eagles never miss their destination
- The ship depends on a small rudder, a man made compass to sail through the seas. Without site of the land probably for days, yet it is safely taken across the seas by a few men and women who directs it to its destination. No one can follow its direct path for there are no highways on the seas.
- We may never understand what pulls a man so strongly to a woman that he is always looking out to be with and please her. When a man is in love with a woman she cannot be wrong, whatsoever she does pleases him.
- The only Begotten Son of God will love us so much to leave His throne in heaven to come down to earth to face the shame of the cross, and shed His blood to reconcile us to the Father. He did not have to do it, but He chose to
- That God chooses to give us so much freedom and liberty to participate in work of redemption by the privilege of preaching the Good News.

With all the power of the angels, they cannot preach the Gospel; neither can they repent once they miss it. The only explanation that we have for all these is that it is GRACE; for by grace are we saved; by His mercies which are new every day, are we kept!

Three Things Go Well and Four Are Comely

Bible Passages: Proverbs 30:29-31; Psalm 147:1; Jeremiah 6:2

Proverbs 30: 29-31
29 There be three things which go well, yea, four are comely...

The Psalmist says praise is comely! Agur the son of Jakeh writer of Proverbs 30 says there are four things which are comely. Jeremiah likens the daughter of Zion to a delicate and comely woman! – Jeremiah 6: 2. The word comely means pleasing in appearance; proper or seemly behavior; or pleasing in appearance and attractive. So if the Word of God through the Psalmist says that praise is comely; and another writer lists four things that are comely to behold.

God is calling our attention to these creatures. What are the features and characteristics that make them to be beautiful to behold? How is praise a proper and seemly behavior?
- The lion does not turn from any one – it is very sure of and confident of its strength. And not intimidated by anything
- The greyhound is fast and does and puts its speed and agility to use in the face of attack by predators
- The he-goat is very persistent in its courtship of female goats and never takes no for an answer!

- The king is so sure of his power and authority that he makes rule and laws and takes charge of the defense of his territory with boldness and confidence! He is confident of the effectiveness his authority and power.

We must walk confidently with our God given grace and authority!

Prayer Point:

Grant me grace to honor God with all of my life.

WEEK 13

YE SEEK JESUS OF NAZARETH ... He is risen!

📖 Bible Passages: Mark 16; Matthew 28; Ecclesiastes 12

Mark 16: 5-7
5 And entering into the sepulcher, they saw a young man sitting on the right side, clothed in a long white garment; and they were affrighted. 6 And he saith unto them, Be not affrighted: Ye seek Jesus of Nazareth, which was crucified: he is risen; he is not here: behold the place where they laid him...

We would wish to ask our young readers physically/spiritually young) as we celebrate the resurrection of our Lord and Savior Jesus Christ, are: -
- Whom/What do you seek?
- Where and where are you seeking?
- How much effort and time are you willing to put into the search?
- Why are you seeking?

Our answers to these questions will determine: -
- How we stand with God, fulfill and enjoy God's plan for our lives
- We must recognize that God has a general plan for humanity, and specific plans, for each and every one of us. Moreover there are assignments for times and seasons of our lives.
- It is only by continually being in touch with Him, by seeking Him, in every affair of our lives that we can know His mind, plan, and purpose for our lives.
- It does not matter when, where on how we are, He is always available and willing to deliver us, set our feet on the path of righteousness
- These early disciples went seeking Him because they were decided to follow the One who met all their needs, and had answers to all their questions. We likewise must we must persevere in our thirst, hunger and desire for Christ.

- The disciples were told that He was no longer in the grave, because HE IS RISEN. Now we have to seek Him through His Spirit – HE LIVES FOR EVER! So; we will always find Him, every time we seek Him.
- Understand that HE LIVES forever, never to die again. As a result of this all things possible for us for as long as we believe. Night comes when no one can work! We must work (seek), while it is day. We will find Him when we seek Him DILIGENTLY and EARLY, with all our heats and mind and soul. Seek Him while He may yet be found! *Remember now thy Creator in days of thy youth....* Ecclesiastes 12:1

Jesus Came To Save and Deliver All!

Bible Passages: John Chapters 3-5

John 3:1-2
1 There was a man of the Pharisees, named Nicodemus, a ruler of the Jews:

At any time and in all places He was ready with a word and a touch. His ministry was not confined to the rich, or to the poor.
- Nicodemus came by night seeking answers... and he found the miracle of the second birth – John 3

The Samaritan woman came for water at the well
- She left to tell her city about the Source of Living Water – John 4
- The paralytic at the pool found out that even 38 years of lameness was not an obstacle to the miracle working Son of God – John 5.
- Jews or Samaritan, religious leader or outcast; the love and compassion of Jesus knows no bounds

Christ Jesus has called us to the ministry of reconciliation that does not discriminate. We are to attend to each person with the same love, compassion and attitude.

This is because Christ Jesus died and rose for every human being. The grace for salvation is available to all.
- The rich needs the Gospel, as much as the poor;
- The learned and intellectual as well as the ignorant and uneducated. The mighty as well as the weak
- The great nations as well as the small or weak ones.

We are to take the Gospel to ALL PEOPLES, not just the POOR NATIONS. In preaching of the Gospel, we must distinguish between dividing the food and sharing the Word. There is need to touch the poor (demonstrate our love by work), by meeting the physical needs. Our goal must always be to reach their souls – for bodily exercise *profited* nothing

Prayer Points:

That I may know Jesus Christ and Him crucified

JOSEPH – A TYPE OF JESUS CHRIST

Some spiritual parallels between the lives of Joseph the man who took Israel to the land of Egypt to avoid the famine in Canaan, and Jesus of Nazareth the Messiah of mankind

Are these parallels only the result of mere coincidence? These parallels make for enjoyable reading and spiritual illumination. For instance:
- The name of Jesus' earthly father was Joseph
- Jesus' chief accuser was Joseph ben Caiaphas
- The man who buried Jesus was Joseph of Arimathea

Parallel Activity	Joseph	Jesus
The favorite son of a wealthy father	Genesis 37:3	Matthew 3:17
He was a shepherd	Genesis 37:2	John 10:11-14
Taken into Egypt to avoid being killed	Genesis. 37:28	Matthew 2:13
Became a servant	Genesis 39:4	Philippians 2:7
Began his ministry at the age of thirty	Genesis 41:46	Luke 3:23
Filled with the Spirit of God	Genesis 41:38	Luke 4:1
Returned good for evil	Genesis 50:20	Matthew 5:44
Humble and unspoiled by wealth	Genesis 45:7-8	John 13:12
Taught by God	Genesis 41:16	John 5:19
Loved people freely	Genesis 45:15	John 13:34
Gained confidence of others quickly	Genesis 39:3	Matthew 8:8
Gave bread to hungry who came to him	Genesis 41:57	Mark 6:41
Resisted most difficult temptations	Genesis 39:8-9	Hebrews 4:15
Given vision into the future	Genesis 37:6	Matt. 24:3
Tested people to reveal their true nature	Genesis 42:25	Mark 11:30
Hated for his teachings	Genesis 37:8	John 7:7
Sold for the price of a slave	Genesis 37:28	Matt. 26:15
He was falsely accused	Genesis 39:14	Mark 14:56
Silent before his accuser	Genesis 39:20	Mark 15:4
Condemned between two prisoners	Genesis 40:2-3	Luke 23:32
Dead before his father	Genesis 37:33	Luke 23:46
Held for two, and free on the third day	Genesis 41:1	Luke 9:22
He arose into a new life	Genesis 41:41	Mark 16:6
He was not recognized by his own brethren	Genesis 42.8	Luke 24:37
He returned to his father	Genesis 46:29	Mark 16:19
He became a lord / Lord	Genesis. 45:8	Revelation. 19:16

WEEKS 14-26

WEEK 14

ONE CAN CHASE A THOUSAND AND TWO TEN!

Bible Passages: Deuteronomy 32:9-31; 2 Kings 6; Matthew 18

Deuteronomy 32: 30-31
30 How should one chase a thousand, and two put ten thousand to flight, except their Rock had sold them, and the LORD had shut them up?...

As with every activity of God, we must consider that He is infinite in His power majesty and glory. He is Providential in His ways, actions and relationships with us finite minds. He does not change, but changes situations and circumstances at His will. Let us consider these facts: -
- Our enemies are mighty
- We are without strength
- Our Redeemer, who fights our battles, is Almighty, and in the power of His might we sure to overcome!

Our human minds may never be able to understand how one person can overcome one thousand; and two overcoming 10, 000. Simple arithmetic can be used to explain two chasing two thousand if one can overcome one thousand, and so on.
But with God it is a different story. When two people are in agreement the host of heaven is put into action to fight on their behalf. Remember that His thoughts are far beyond ours and His ways past finding.
Moreover as we walk with God, we must remember that our enemy who is also God's is consistently coming against us with his host. But the host of heaven who is more than that of the enemy is always battle ready to fight for us for as long as we abide in His will, that is agree with Him.

Jesus told us in that when two of us shall agree as touching an issue it shall be done by our Father in heaven. Here we see Jesus showing the key to victory and receiving from God – Matthew 18: 19. We also see Jesus sending the disciples out in twos to preach the Gospel – Luke 10: 11; and we see Jesus giving instructions as to how they were to conduct themselves as they went.

We can do all things, through Christ, for His ways are not our ways, and His thoughts far beyond ours. So when we agree with God concerning His plans for our lives, and when we agree with other believers the outcome of our victory is beyond imagination. TEAM UP WITH SOMEONE TODAY!

Jehoshaphat's Unusual Victory Arsenal

Bible Passages: 2 Chronicles 20; Joshua 6; Acts 16

2 Chronicles 20: 1-37 *1 It came to pass after this also, that the children of Moab, and the children of Ammon, and with them other beside the Ammonites, came against Jehoshaphat to battle....*

As believers we are daily confronted with battles, because our adversary the devil, as Peter puts it, is roaring like a lion, looking for whom he will devour – 1 Peter 5: 8. God expects us to live victoriously, and in abundance at all times.

God wants us to be above principalities, powers, and all the situations that they create or cause. Have you ever considered this episode, when a whole nation went to battle, with the choir not the generals, nor the sharp-shooters leading? It happened and the nation of Judah came back with the spoils of war! Then to be able to triumph over every attack and opposition we are follow the example of Jehoshaphat:

- Acknowledge that there is a problem and that we are helpless and so we need help.
- Knowing that our help comes from God, who is able to save completely.
- Realize that the same God who delivered others can also rescue us and then
- Come to Him humbly and reverently with a determination to make our requests known to Him.

He knows our needs, but He demands that we ask! We are to call on Him; be willing to obey His instructions even when they are not logical. There was a precedent for Jehoshaphat. Joshua on God's unusual strategy led the children of Israel into the Promised Land.

The wall of Jericho fell and the city was delivered into the hands of Joshua and the children of Israel. It is not about the physical weapon or strength that determines the direction of the battle.

<u>Prayer Points</u>:

Dear LORD please help me to overcome every opposition to my life.

WEEK 15

THE VALUE OF INSTRUCTIONS

Bible Passages: Proverbs 12; 22; Romans 3-6; Titus 1-3

Proverbs 12: 1-6
1 Whoso loveth instruction loveth knowledge: but he that hateth reproof is brutish.
2 A good man obtaineth favor of the LORD: ...

Truly our God is a God of order, and gave parents and adults the privilege to train and bring up the little ones, to be led in the way of the LORD; thereby they can know the will and purpose of God for their lives. That is are able to make the right choices when they are old enough to; for each one must make a choice between life and death!

Each person must come to the realization that he/she is a sinner, repent and receive Jesus as Lord and savior, pick up his/her cross and follow Jesus, because each one is accountable for him/herself! Before the age of accountability, God strategically place others who have been through the stage we are in, to lift up our hands as we proceed in the journey of life. So:

- There is need for instruction, we do not always know, what is right, and when we do know we still need the Lord to help us to follow through. As leaders, parents or adults we must be willing to lead the younger ones in the right direction; with the understanding that you can only give out of what you have.. But Good instruction is valuable only when it is followed; we must be followers of Christ even in learning from others.

- The Holy Spirit is our Chief Instructor and Teacher. He is always available to lead us into, and show us new things as we allow Him. He also corrects us when we make mistakes.
- God has also given us men and women who can lead us in the right direction, in life. His ways and instructions are perfect and eternal, we are temporal, but if we allow our spirits to have the final say in the affairs of our lives, then we will be wise!

And the Child Samuel Grew ....

Bible Passages: 1 Samuel 2; 3: 19-21; Hebrews 8:

1 Samuel 2: 26 *And the child Samuel grew on, and was in favor both with the LORD, and also with men.*

We see in these Scriptures, that God was with Samuel, right from the time he was a child even when he was not in a position to recognize the voice of God by himself. We can attribute Samuel's success and greatness in life to the following:
- God was with Him – We must receive God's mercy with gratitude – He told Moses as reaffirmed in Romans 9: 15-16, He has the prerogative of mercy.
- He had a praying mother – truly, God is gracious and merciful, but He is a just God, and has decreed that we must pray in order us to receive from Him
- We have a responsibility as parents and children and children of God, to pray for our children, siblings, family, neighbors and other people if we truly love them and desire that changes come to their lives and situations –

- Prayer not only changes, it also keeps things. It shows our trust and dependence on God. Moreover it is one of the armor that we need to constantly put on in order to defeat the devil and his cohorts as they work against us. God wants to commune with us no matter our age or disposition, it is our responsibility to desire to and be ready to receive from Him.
- We can act only what we hear, see or touch. To be able to see, hear, and touch God, we must do so by faith, and allow the Holy Spirit to commune with us. Are you in tune with God?

You can tell how you stand with God through His Word. We must choose to abide and trust God to play His part. We are predestined to grow in spirit and stature – We still must work out our salvation.

Prayer Point:

Deliverance from bad habits and evil thoughts.

WEEK 16

THEY THAT WAIT UPON THE LORD...

Bible Passages: Isaiah 40: 1 – 31; Joshua 1414

Isaiah 40: 31 *But they that wait upon the LORD shall renew their strength; they shall mount up with wings as eagles; they shall run, and not be weary; and they shall walk, and not faint.*

The Bible refers to the bird eagle twenty three times in twenty-three different verses. The eagle is a very agile bird with very keen eyes, a very efficient predator and very accurate in hunting for and capturing its prey. It is also noted for its patience in waiting for the appearance of its prey.

One of the peculiar things about the eagle is that it also constantly sheds its old feathers, during which time it oils its bruised body and waits for the growth of brand new feathers that can take it to all the great heights it has to fly. It needs good and well organized feathers to maintain the heights it attains in flights.

Therefore it is important for us to take notice of what God is telling us through His prophet – Isaiah that if we can patiently wait for God's timing in all our endeavors, no matter how long or how painful. One of the enduring qualities of a Christian is to be able to persist and persevere in receiving promises and gifts from God. We must understand that to everything there is time. It is our responsibility to be able to wait for God's timing which is always right and perfect.

Just like the eagle no matter how old we may be in age, nor the experiences we have had in life, we will be able to say like Caleb – *"Now therefore give me this mountain..."* Joshua 14: 12.

God expects us to persist, persevere and trust Him to do what He promised us, not withstanding what the prevailing circumstances are saying.

He promised to give us the strength to wait and endure the difficult situations that we may be facing; to give us the peace that passes all understanding; that implies that our peace is guaranteed irrespective of the turmoil and uproar going on around us.

We can enjoy His peace and assurance, when we make Him the object of our worship, that is when there is no other God but Him. If He truly is number one in our lives every challenge will be seen as stepping stones to breakthrough and greatness.

The People That Do Know...

Bible Passages: Daniel 11: 32; Hosea 4: 6; Luke 6

Daniel 11: *32 And such as do wickedly against the covenant shall he corrupt by flatteries: but the people that do know their God shall be strong, and do exploits.*

Through the Scriptures we know that the degree to which we are privileged to know about God and the aspect of Himself that God reveals to us determines the extent and the area of the blessing, breakthrough or success that we have from Him God demands that we know His nature and character.

He is a God of Providence and no one can query why or what He does. However there is a demand placed on us as Believers to seek Him consciously and to consistently search the Scriptures to know more of Him, as we walk with Him through the enabling of the Holy Spirit.

We are the product of our thoughts, and our thoughts emanate from our hearts; and are influenced by how much of God we have in us – out of the abundance of the heart the mouth speaks forth. Remember with the mouth confession is made unto salvation.

God created us in His image and gave us authority and ability to have dominion over all other creatures; this status which was lost as a result of the fall of Adam.

When we become born again, we are empowered to step into our position of authority, of establishing the kingdom of God here on earth. This can be done by knowing His plans purposes and timing for the things that we require from Him. This involves:
- Casting down every imagination
- Bringing every thought to obedience in Christ Jesus
- Pulling down every strong hold and every high thing that exalts itself against the knowledge of our God.
- Prepared and ready to revenge every form of disobedience and completely obeying God.

These can be achieved by knowing the will and God. It is only by knowing and doing the will of God can you do exploits through Christ Jesus.

Prayer Points:

To walk in the Light of the Word and Will of God

WEEK 17

THE POWER OF THE TONGUE!

Bible Passages: Proverbs 15; 18: 21; James 1: 26-3:5-9; 1Peter 3

Proverbs 18: 21 *Death and life are in the power of the tongue: and they that love it shall eat the fruit thereof*
James 3: 5-9

The tongue is a vital part of the body by which communicate our thoughts wishes and desires to God and fellow beings. It is a link between our inner being and the outside world. In the physical it is very important in the grinding and swallowing of food and water which are important to our physically being alive.

In the Spiritual realm too, the tongue is very important, for God spoke creation into existence by faith, and we are made in the image of God; we are empowered to speak our breakthroughs and achievements into existence by faith.

We must remember however that out of the abundance of the heart the mouth speaks forth. The question then is what is in your heart? God only listens to and honors His word. Knowing this then the starting point for progress, achievement and success in life must be the Word of God, which is also the will of God.

No wonder the devil confronted Eve with the question – *Has God said?* And He told Jesus, what God said concerning the Son of God – *He will give His angels charge...* We must understand that God has not sent us to defend His word, or to engage in discussion with the devil. Rather we are to resist him, with the Word, by the power of the Holy Spirit.

- Jesus responded to the devil's challenge by using the Word of God – Deuteronomy 8: 3; Matthew 4: 4; Luke 4: 4. We must learn complete obedience to God and His word; yielding our lives to Jesus the only way by which we can be saved;
- As we present His Word to Him by faith in total submission to His will for our lives, God responds to our situation here on earth – Note that He does not desire that any one should perish, but that all will come to repentance.
- If He cares for the sparrow, He cares for you so use your tongue wisely! So that it may be well with us He demands that we use our tongues wisely, by speaking His word; remember that out of the abundance of the heart the mouth speaks. So fill your heart with the Word of God.

That It May Be Well With Thee!

Bible Passages: Deuteronomy 6: Romans 7-8; Zechariah 4

Deuteronomy 6: 2- 3
2 That thou mightest fear the LORD thy God, to keep all his statutes and his commandments, which I command thee, thou, and thy son, and thy son's son...

Several times I (Margaret), like many other believers have pondered why the law was given to the children of Israel.

They were asked to pass it on from one generation to the other. Notice also that the believers are given a mandate to preach the Good News of the life, death and resurrection of Jesus Christ. This is by telling others of the only living way to God through the atoning blood of the Lamb, so that believing all can be saved.

As has been or will be pointed out severally in this piece God created us in His image and desires fellowship with us – Genesis 3:8; so when man fell He activated so to speak the machinery of the process of redemption which He has planned before man even came to the scene! The journey from the fall of the first Adam to that of the Second was long, but sure and guaranteed.

It went through a series of revelations of His ways, nature and character, and requirements from us to various men and women of all ages.

From the institution of the priesthood, to the kingdom and the era of the prophets God has been constant in His will and plan for humanity. So when we become born again, we have a responsibility to find out what we need to do so that *it might be well* with us.

We are to trust God to empower us to do even the things that are humanly speaking impossible to accomplish. That is why Paul's admonition refreshing – *Let the weak say I am strong.* - Have faith in God!

Prayer Point:

To have power over my tongue and flesh

WEEK 18

THE FRUIT OF THE SPIRIT- PATIENCE

Bible Passages: Galatians 5: 22-24; James 1: 1-4

Galatians 5: 22-24
22 But when the Holy Spirit controls our lives, he will produce this kind of fruit in us: joy, peace, patience, kindness, goodness, faithfulness
23 Gentleness and self-control Here there is no conflict with the law ... NLT

One of the ways by which we know someone has been touched by the love of Jesus Christ, is the change that comes to the life of that person. This is within, but shows with outward manifestations. The way by which people know that one is a true follower of Jesus is in the fruit of the Spirit.

If the Holy Spirit dwells in us and we allow Him to work the work of salvation in every area of our lives there must be an evidence of His presence. This is itemized in Galatians 5: 22-24. Patience, when allowed to spring forth in our lives is like a life guard who in order to save a person, first allows him/her to be filled with so much water that he/she becomes helpless and must totally depend on the life guard to be rescued from downing.

The life guard has to patiently wait (despite his activity in the water to keep afloat) until the drowning person can no longer save him/her self. Apostle James tells us that the trial of our faith works patience. Job patiently waited on God to change the situation of his life – Job 14: 14.

This is by learning to keep our focus on God, who is able to make the necessary changes at the appointed, time.

This is when we will give Him all the glory, all will testify boldly as Moses reported in Deuteronomy 32: 31 *For their rock is not as our Rock, even our enemies themselves being judges.*

So let us consider these there two as we depend on God to empower us to bear fruit in our Christian walk:

- Mary the mother of Jesus patiently bore her shame as she carried Jesus in her womb and nurtured Him so that the Savior of mankind could be born. He must be born, before He could go to the cross; and He must go to the cross to save us; for without the shedding of the blood there is no remission of sins!
- Christ Jesus bore the shame of the cross so that humanity could be reconciled to God.

God is interested in all generations. He makes His grace available to all. We must be will to accept not just the gift of salvation, but the empowerment by the Holy Spirit to bear enduring fruit, part of which is patience.

Of Vision and Perception

Bible Passages: Matthew 13:14; Mark 4; 8

Mark 4: 11-12
11 And he said unto them, Unto you it is given to know the mystery of the kingdom of God: but unto them that are without, all these things are done in parables..

It is not enough to give or provide light; there must be eye to see the light and the objects it shines on. It is not enough to see the light; there must be a mind to know the identity the objects the light shines on; that is perceive the true nature of such objects; see them as they reflect the light according to their composition

He did not just give us the Holy Spirit to help us perceive; He gave us the Holy Spirit to keeps us in the Light, so we do not stumble in the darkness of the world; that way we are able to stand in Him; it is in standing that we enjoy the liberty in and the warmth in the Light

God is willing to keep us in the Light, if we choose to; for abiding in Him depends also on our choice Our choice is based on our perception of Him and His Word.

We must see Him able to keep and transform us; and have the right perception of ourselves; for as a man thinks in his heart, so is he; We must accept His Word and testimony of who we are and who He can make us to be, for He is Almighty.

The steps are simple and must be followed simply; accept His verdict of who you are and who you can become. Accept His call of repentance; that is from darkness to light We must trust Him to keep us in His Light, at all times.

To abide in His Light, is an eternal hope by choice soberly and sincerely made; kept alive consciously and humbly through grace, by faith, sustained with genuine and unconditional love.

Prayer Point:

To know and understand God as He deals with me

WEEK 19

THANKSGIVING – Not an Option!

Bible Passages: 1, 2 Thessalonians; 1 & 2 Timothy & Philemon

Psalm 68: *19 Blessed be the Lord, who daily loadeth us with benefits, even the God of our salvation. Selah*
2 Corinthians *11:25...thrice I suffered shipwreck, a night and a day I have...*

Thanksgiving is the process whereby, one in gratitude expresses appreciation, for a benefit or favor; that is the expression of thankfulness for blessings received from another individual. There is a necessity for us to give thanks at all time to the Almighty God, who daily loads us with benefits – Thanksgiving is the:-
- Result of the Spirit-filled life – Ephesians 5: 18-20.
- Result of the Word-filled life
- Key to our prayer life
- Imperative to a Christian's walk with God
- Therapeutic releasing the soul from hurt and fear

Thanksgiving results in victorious living. Reading through the epistles of Paul, we see a man who was filled with thanksgiving, despite his life being filled with so many difficulties.

He was stoned at Lystra, driven out of Thessalonica and his ministry destroyed. He was rejected by the Athenians in Athens, jailed at Philippi; twice in shipwreck. The Bible carefully links the spirit of gratitude to victorious living – 1 Corinthians 15: 57; 2 Corinthians 2: 14.

It should be a lifestyle rather than an event. As Christians we are called to give thanks at all times. Subsequently the ability to rejoice comes out of a lifestyle of thanksgiving.

Hence we can follow Paul's injunction in Philippians 4: 4. It is not only when we have positive results that we are to give thanks. David the king and sweet Psalmist of Israel is also a good example of someone who exhibited this attitude. Whether he was making a request to God, or battling his enemies, he always had time to thank God for past and future blessings; to praise and worship God for who He is.

Thanksgiving causes us to refocus attention away from ourselves and challenges and to redirect them to God, who in the first instance should be number one in our lives! In some parts of Africa, there is a special little berry called taste berry. It changes the taste of everything making them sweet and pleasant.

The attitude of gratitude is the Christian's little berry! When the attitude of gratitude becomes a part of our being, it turns every sour thing to sweet. Like all other aspects of our relationship with God we must choose to do what He requires from us and He will enable us to accomplish. WHAT IS YOUR CHOICE?

The Sun And The Moon Praise Him!

Bible Passages: Psalm 148; 1 Corinthians 15; 2 Corinthians 2; Philippians 4

Philippians 4: 4 *Rejoice in the Lord alway: and again I say, Rejoice.*

The need for Believers to continually praise God cannot be over emphasized. He primarily created us for His praise and then He demands praise and thanksgiving from us. Moreover it is good for our spirit soul and body.

It is generally observed that people who are joyous, speaks well of others and are appreciative are often easier to relate with and less prone to some ailments such and cancer, high blood pressure and some others.

Whether we praise Him or not, God is not in short supply of creatures to continually praise Him, both in the heavens and in the earth.

Though we are commanded to, it is still a privilege to be able to do so. The Bible very carefully links the spirit of gratitude to victorious Christian living –Thanksgiving should be a lifestyle rather than an event.

As Christians we are called to give thanks at all times. Subsequently the ability to rejoice comes out of a lifestyle of thanksgiving. Hence we can follow Paul's injunction in It is not only when we have good harvest or positive results that we are to give thanks.

David is a good example of someone who exhibited this attitude. Whether he was making a request to God, or battling his enemies, he always had time to thank God for past and future blessings.

Thanksgiving causes us to change the object of our focus and attention from ourselves, others, issues and challenges and redirect them to God, who in the first instance should be number one in our lives!

Prayer Points:

To see more of God and less of myself

WEEK 20

HANNAH'S PERCEPTIONS OF GOD

Bible Passages: 1 Samuel 1:10-11; 2: 1-10; Job 13:

Before the Birth of Samuel
1 Samuel 1: 10-11
1 10 And she was in bitterness of soul, and prayed unto the LORD, and wept sore...

Hannah at this time knew God as the LORD of Hosts – The Jehovah Sabboath; that is the God who goes to, and fights, our battles for us. She with this simple but powerful knowledge of God, went to Shiloh to demand that God fights her battles of:
- Barreness
- Shame and ridicule from her rival Peninnah;
- Sadness and sorrow from year to hear;
- Insult from Eli, who thought and accused her of being drunk while she was praying.

After the Birth of Samuel
1 Samuel 2: 1-10
1 There is none holy as the LORD: for there is none beside thee: neither is there any rock like our God.

When Hannah, brought Samuel to Shiloh she expressed the following about God; this revealed a greater and more glorious perception of the God who answered her prayers.
- The Only true God, for there is none like Him;
- The LORD our Rock;
- The God of knowledge;
- By Him actions are weighed – The Judge;
- He is solid and strong like a rock;
- He fights our battles and assures victory;

- He is the Provider of all good things;
- He can make and unmake everything and everyone;
- He owns the earth, the sustenance of which is depended on Him

What is Your Perception of God?

Bible Passages: 1 Samuel 1:10-11; 2: 1-10; Job 13: 15-16; 1 Corinthians 10: 11
God demands that we have the right perspective of Him
Know Him;
- Trust in Him;
- Have faith in Him;
- Abide in Christ;
- Follow Him;
- Obey Him; irrespective of the challenges we face

We must understand though that He is the One who reveals Himself to us. It is not enough to know Him, it is important and vital that we chose to follow and obey Him, irrespective of what is going on around us. He desires that we, like Job and all who have experienced His salvation, deliverance, protection and provision among other blessing to be able to say – Job 13:15-16
15 Though he slay me, yet will I trust in him: but I will maintain mine own ways before him...

The Scriptures were written to serve as examples to us – *1 Corinthians 10:11; so that we by faith can know God, the same way Hannah perceived Him not only before but after her miracle.*

Prayer Points:

Reveal Yourself to me dear at all times and in all situations and circumstances of my life.

WEEK 21

DAVID, SAUL, JONATHAN, AND MEPHIBOSHETH

Bible Passages: 1 Samuel 24; 31; 2 Samuel 4: 4; 9: 1-13; 1 Kings 9; 1 Chronicles 10; Matthew 1: 1-18

2 Samuel 9: 7-13
7 *And David said unto him, Fear not: for I will surely shew thee kindness for Jonathan thy father's sake, and will restore thee all the land of Saul thy father; and thou shalt eat bread at my table continually...*

DAVID

The sweet Psalmist of Israel, the man after God's own heart. God Himself bye passed all protocols to anoint him king over Israel even when there was still a reigning king!

God called David a man after His heart. He was full of praise and acknowledgement for God's blessings and ready to repent whenever he missed it, with assurance of God's love and forgiveness.

David was loyal to Saul, and did not kill him even when he had the opportunities to do so. He was loyal to his friend Jonathan, making his son Mephibosheth's to sit at table with, and showed kindness even to Mephibosheth's servants.

Through David the kingdom of Israel prospered; he walked diligently with God and whenever he missed it he repented and made amends. His commitment and dedication to God was genuine.

The Messiah was destined to come through his lineage. Through the lives of these four men in the Bible, let us consider these questions?. Where do you choose to stay? Is it on the battlefield with the dethroned king? Would you choose to be at table with the established king?

SAUL

He was the first king of Israel. He had a choice and a privilege to establish his lineage to rule in Israel, but his rebellion and inability to adapt to the necessity of sharing power and popularity led to his doom. He allowed jealousy to take the better part of him as he pursued the life of David, rather than the governance of the people of God.

He allowed his flesh to h\rule over his life, thereby choosing to kill one of the very people he was appointed to protect and govern! He did not get the right perception of the call of God upon his life, and chose to obey the people of God rather than God and his servant (Prophet Samuel).

He took on the responsibility if the prophet and priest of God for which he was not called, nor qualified. He died with his sons and children in battle

JONATHAN

Jonathan was the eldest son of Saul, and a very loyal friend of David. Under normal circumstances he would have inherited the throne from his father Saul after his demise. Jonathan acknowledged that God has chosen and was with David instead of his father, yet he stuck to his father.

He knew the times and the plans of God for Israel and David, but made the wrong choice of staying with his father who was already rejected by God. It is not enough to know God's Word, plans and purposes; we are expected to make the wise decisions from such knowledge. He died in battle at Mount Gilboa with his father and two of his brothers.

- It is not enough to know God's will, we must follow
- Partial obedience is as good as disobedience.
- God judges us by our actions based on the revealed knowledge of Him that we have – To whom much is given, much is expected

MEPHIBOSHETH

He was five years old when his father Jonathan and his grandfather Saul died on Mount Gilboa in the Battle of Jezreel. He fell and became paralyzed when his nurse heard the outcome of the battle, feared for his life and fled with him to protect him. Despite this disability he still had his royal treatment with his servants intact.

Although Mephibosheth was often wronged and his life filled with many challenges, he never grew angry or bitter. He was loyal to David and showed an understanding of the word and plans of God for the house of David. He was privileged to be invited to live in the palace, wine and dine with King David in recognition of his father Jonathan's loyalty.

Unlike his father Jonathan, he chose to at table with the established king rather than the inheritance from the last doomed kingdom.

Prayer Point: To make the right choices and decisions

WEEK 22

CHOOSE ... WHOM YOU WILL SERVE....

Bible Passages: Joshua 24: 1-33; John 1: 12; 2 Corinthians 9: 7

Life is about choices. Accepting Jesus as Lord and Savior is a choice that every believer had to make. Joshua here presented the Israelites the same choice we are presented with today: Reverence the LORD as the sole object of our worship.
- Serve him – By obeying His commands.
- In sincerity – The whole heart in His worship.
- And in truth – According to the directions He gave in His infallible word.
- Put away the gods, listed by Joshua as those:
  – That their fathers worshipped on the other side of Jordan that is the gods of the Chaldeans – fire, light, and sun.
  – Of the Egyptians, Apis, Anubis, the ape, serpents, vegetables, etc.
  – Of the Canaanites, Moabites, or Baal-peor etc

It is astonishing that like the Israelites in the days of Joshua despite all that God has done and doing for us people still turn to idols after they have experienced the goodness of the LORD – Amos 5:26; Acts 7:41. Images and symbols cannot represent the Divine, so we cannot profess to worship God through the images as has been alleged by some Christians known for image worship.
No images –Exodus 20: 4.

Choose you this day whom ye will serve –
- All service that was not free and voluntary could be only deceit and hypocrisy, and *God loves a cheerful giver*. Joshua therefore calls on them to make their choice, for God himself would not force any one. If we must serve Him at we must choose to do so with all our hearts
- The choice must be made now; tomorrow may be too late – Hebrew 3: 7-14. Joshua and family chose JEHOVAH as their portion. God expects that we reach our family members and nurture them in Christ.
- Consistently as believers we are confronted with choices even in the daily affairs of our lives; we must rely on God for help in making every decision.

I and the Children... We are for wonders

Bible Passages: Isaiah 8: 18; Hosea 1;Acts 10

Isaiah 8: *18 Behold, I and the children whom the LORD hath given me are for signs and for wonders in Israel...*

Names of children were often emblematic and the prophets themselves were regarded as signs of important events – Ezekiel 24: 24; Isaiah 20: 3. The names given them were intended to teach important lessons to the people of Israel; quoted with reference to the Messiah in Hebrews 2: 1 3.

Their names were significant, and designed to illustrate some truth . They were to inculcate the truth in regard to the presence and protection of God.

- Immanuel, 'God with us,' Isaiah 7:14; Shear-jashub, 'the remnant shall return,' Isaiah 7:3, none but God could be the protector of the nation.
- And in like manner, it is possible that his name Isaiah – signifying the salvation of Jehovah, had been given him with such a reference. Well, it was a name which would remind them of the truth that he was now inculcating, that salvation was to be found in Yahweh, and that they should look to him.

The early Christians were so first called at Antioch because the things they did. God expects that not just our physical names but our character and attitude to portray the God whose name we bear. Each one must make a choice to serve God in truth:
- Cain and Abel; one of the sins of Cain was that he chose not to be responsible for his brother safety; but killed him– Genesis 4: 9.
- Cornelius brought his household to hear Peter preach the Gospel – Acts 10.
- The jailer with Paul and Silas got his household to hear the Gospel and they all were saved – Acts 16.

We must arise to our responsibilities to our family members; by seeing to their salvation and maturity in Christ. We are also required to bring forth spiritual children and nurture them in the fear of the LORD, so that they too can operate in the power of God.

Prayer Point: My life and family be a wonder to all

WEEK 23

IT IS BY THE SPIRIT OF THE LORD

Bible Passages: Zechariah 4; Daniel 2; Philippians 4; Romans 9

Zechariah 4: 6
Then he answered and spake unto me, saying, This is the word of the LORD unto Zerubbabel, saying, Not by might, nor by power, but by my spirit, saith the LORD of hosts

The Christian journey or race is full of challenges, obstacles and hindrances along its path. Some as a result of human actions and, or inactions orchestrated by the Devil and his cohorts to distract us from achieving our goals in life; sometimes coming at us through human agents; but allowed of God who being a Just One, will not break his Law.

However, no matter the level of our advancement in the race or maturity in our walk with God, we are equipped to resist the devil and be able to achieve every purpose of God for our lives. This we see in the lives of the Old Testament saints and we see Jesus demonstrate to us both by His Example and in the instructions He gave that we see the New Testament Christians operate in.

One basic truth that we must know is that we are not alone and that in our physical strength we cannot accomplish anything; but with God we CAN DO ALL THINGS.

No matter the things that we have to accomplish, we must know that it is by grace and the mercies of God that we can even have the thought of doing such things.

The ability and the enablement to accomplish them is at the prerogative of God the Father through Christ Jesus and perfected by the Holy Spirit. We are not to focus on the obstacles that will be removed but the God who cannot be moved; and does not change – Malachi 3: 6. This leaves us with the option of trusting, and acknowledging God every all the way.

Also no matter where we find ourselves whether in the valley, in the plains or at the mountain top, God's plan and purpose will surely come to pass – 2 Corinthians 9: 8.

The Holy Spirit who indwells us enable us to mature in Christ, bear abiding fruits, preach the Good News with signs and wonders, and establish the kingdom of God right here on earth.

I Believe... That Whosoever...

Bible Passages: Mark 9; John 9; 11; Acts 27; 2 Corinthians 4: 13

The questions that we all must answer are: What do you believe? Or who do you believe? Our response to these questions determines the extent to which we can enjoy our walk with God. Our beliefs are shaped by what we hear, see and experience.

But the responsibility to believe and act on what we believe is a choice that each person must make in life. God presents us with his promises both:-

General – As in the issue of salvation which comes by believing in His Son Jesus Christ came to the world.

He was crucified, died, buried and rose from the dead that we may no longer be subject to law of sin and death

Specific – Example of specific issues of our lives – Paul was assured by the angel of God that he and those with him in the ship will not perish in the sea as they sailed towards Rome.

Paul had a divine mission, and a purpose for going to Rome. The sailors were not did not follow Paul's instructions as to when to set sail. He called on and relied on God for safety, and since God's purpose must be fulfilled, his request was granted and as always God's will prevailed.

After salvation comes the issue of learning to walk with and depend on God to keep us in Him. It is those who believe to the end that are saved.

However when there are needs in our lives and in the lives of our neighbors, we are to take those issues to God, who wishes that we prosper and be in health – 3 John 2.

He is interested in every aspect of our lives both now and in the life to come. Whatever may be your need today; take it to God in prayer knowing that Jesus is the resurrection and the life, and

He gives life in abundance now and always. You must come to Him believing. He responds to our faith. – Go to God in prayer not wavering or doubting His Word! You will discover He is expecting you to come!

Prayer Points:

To be empowered to accomplish

WEEK 24

KNOWING GOD...

THE JEHOVAH SHAMMA –The LORD Is There!

Bible Passages: Ezekiel 37; 48: 35; Psalm 23; Romans 10: 11-17

Romans 10: 11-17
... *13 For whosoever shall call upon the name of the Lord shall be saved*
14... and how shall they believe in him of whom they have not heard.........

Our experience of the love of God is conditioned upon his moral and spiritual attributes, and our trust of Him related to our knowledge of Him. When the Psalmist says *Thou art with me –Psalm 23: 4,* he was affirming the presence of Jehovah Shammah – "The LORD is here" One of the greatest gifts we have from God along with the gift of salvation is His presence. Here is a list of some of the confirmation of His presence in the lives of those who walked with Him in Scriptures: -

- God promised Moses His presence when He commissioned Moses to lead the children of Israel out of Egypt – Exodus 3: 2
- God promised Joshua He would be with him wherever he went as he led Israel into the Promised Land and apportioned the land to the tribes of Israel
- When Jesus gave His disciples the great commission, He promised– Matthew 28: 20.

- Knowing that the Jehovah Shammah is always with us, is assuring especially when we encounter loneliness, weariness, disappointments and we feel like giving up, because of the pressures of life.
- When it seems as if no one understands or cares for us, we must be assured that the Ever Present God the Jehovah Shamma is there with us.
- When two or more are gathered in the name of the Jehovah Shammah, He is there is present promised by Jesus. We do not have to see or feel, we must behave with assurance trusting Him to keep His word of always there with us – David understood this and declares that even in the depths of the earth God is there with him.
- Do you belong to Jesus? Much as He wants us to desire Him, He is the One who draws to Himself, for no one can come to Him except He draws.

He Sent His Angel...

Bible Passages: Daniel 6; Mark 8: 1-36; Psalm 31:

In the execution of God's Word on earth it is always His prerogative to choose whatever instrument or medium that He pleases; because He is Sovereign. We must learn to have faith in Him to perform His counsel no matter the situation confronting us, whether we make it physically alive or not, we do not have anything to lose by trusting Him.

Rather we have everything to gain; He rewards diligence and faith in Him. Our sole responsibility is to trust and obey Him at all times, in all situations and at all places.

Daniel knew this, so he worshipped God continually, irrespective of the king's decree and the opposition against him. God demands that we worship Him at all times, irrespective of what we are facing; not putting our lives before His worship. From the Psalmist we know that our times are in His hands.

Daniel chose to defy the orders of king Darius because they run contrary to those of God and he was ready to face the consequences – God is the Supreme Judge who can destroy the flesh and condemn the soul; the earthly king has authority only over the flesh.

Jesus reminded us that there is no profit for anyone who gains the whole world and loses his soul – Mark 8: 36. It is foolishness to deny God in order to save our lives, knowing, we owe Him every breath of them.

Whom do you trust to keep your life? Jesus is the only one who can keep all that is committed into His hands. Daniel depended on God who chose to send His angels to close the mouths of the lions in the den. As we trust Him, God keeps and fulfills His promises
- No cross, no crown;
- No examination, no promotion;
- No test, no testimony *et c.*

<u>Prayer Point</u>:

For God will stir up my faith by His mercy.

WEEK 25

UNDERSTANDING GOD

Bible Passages: Jeremiah 33: 3; Matthew 7: 1-14

Jeremiah 33: 3 *Call to me and I will answer you and show you great and mighty things, which you do not know* (NIV)

Understanding God means to know:
- How He works, and the ways He relates to us;
- His reasons and motivations behind His actions

When we begin to understand God's ways, which are past finding – that is we can never know all His ways but those He reveals to us as we consistently seek Him; then we begin to trust Him more fully. This is because He always has our best interest at heart. Getting to know the heart of God is the greatest adventure one can ever undertake as a follower of Christ.

The place to begin to understand the ways of God more fully is through the study of the His Word. As we immerse ourselves in the Scriptures, we are reading the will and purpose of God for our lives and His creatures including humanity of all ages.

The Holy Spirit reveals the truth to our hearts and minds, when we are receptive to Him, for He will not impose Himself on us.

God desires and demands that we know His will for our lives in order to prosper. In the Old Testament days the people had to rely on the priests to read the Scriptures for them, and on the prophets to tell them the mind of God. He expects us to individually seek Him. All who seek Him finds Him, and if we seek Him diligently we will not miss out on His plans for. When we commit to the study of the Word of God we are prepared for or position:
- Unparalleled intimacy with God
- Ability to see life through the eyes of God
- Patience and peace with God
- Orderly achieving God's plan and purposes Therefore let us as believers learn to spend quality time on God's Word; thereby we will not be found wanting when we face the trials and tribulations of life; especially when the devil comes with his suggestions and temptations – Jesus countered him with the Word of God.

How much of God's word do you have in you? It is sharper than any two edged sword, a valuable weapon against our unrelenting enemy – Hebrews 12: 4.

I Was Glad When They Said Unto Me....

Bible Passages: Psalm 122; Psalm 23

Jerusalem is in the heart of the Holy Land. It is the city of God, where Jesus walked, prayed, and was crucified buried rose again and ascended to heaven. He did many miracles and taught many lessons.

There was a need for peace, and so today like in the time of the Psalmist, we must *Pray for the peace of Jerusalem*. This city has experienced more wars than most, yet no habitation has ever been less peaceful. This new city does not need the sun or the moon for the glory of God and the Lamb are the light.

Jesus told the early disciples as they came back to Him and reported that the devils were subject to them in the name of Jesus – Luke 10: 17, Jesus responded that they should rejoice more in that their names were written in heaven, that that God recons with them.

The most important thing is that, that is our final destination; that is the Home towards which we journey. This should cause us to rejoice. No wonder Paul admonishes us to rejoice always – Philippians 4: 4; in Romans 10:10-14

We are the temples of the LORD, for He no longer dwells in earthen vessels, and if we must follow His word to be glad when going to His house, then we are to be glad at all times, everywhere, and in all situations.

No matter the challenges we face He is always in and with us; so we let us always be joyful because the Source of our joy indwells us. What better testimony do we have to show Him to the world than the one we carry everywhere we go – our countenance, attitude and character – The word *character* is derived from *CHRIST LIKE!* Are you?

Prayer Point: That I may reflect the glory of the LORD

WEEK 26

HAVE YOU TRIED PRAISE?

Bible Passages: Psalm 135; 138; Psalm 16: 11; Luke 11: 1-13

Psalm 135: 1-2

1 Praise ye the LORD, Praise ye the name of the LORD; praise hi, O ye servants of the LORD
2 Ye that stand in the house of the LORD, in the courts of the house of the LORD

For us mortals there is a tendency to approach and call on God, when we desire changes in our lives, by praying to Him. Even unbelievers and agnostics have been proved to call on the name of the LORD when in trouble. As the first disciples went about with Jesus through the nooks and corners of Jerusalem and Israel in those days, they must have noticed one thing about Him the effectiveness of His prayers.

And the authority with which He addressed the issues and met the needs of ALL that called on Him. God has ALL the answer to ALL the questions of our lives. However let us consider one of the points that Jesus raised as He taught the disciples that were with Him and is still teaching us through His written Word today – Luke 11: 2... *Thy kingdom come, Thy will be dome, as in heaven so in earth...*

In heaven God is ceaselessly praised, worshipped and adored. So if we must see God manifested in our lives and situations, we must choose to do as it is done in heaven. That is praise Him without ceasing! We are expected to give thanks in all things.

There are no complaints, and there is complete obedience in heaven! Each being in heaven stays in the position for which he is created, each one fulfilling destiny without questions.

The creature/clay cannot dictate to the Creator/Porter. How do you fair? The angels, the host of heaven and indeed the whole universe bow down to worship the LORD; since God inhabits the praises of His people it follows that we will enjoy heaven here on earth if we choose to consistently and continually praise Him. We and our situations will eventually come to an end, but God and His Word abide forever!

So let us allow our spirits that will eternally live with God experience heaven here on earth as we completely trust and obey Him, praising and acknowledging that He cares about us, knows what we are going through and can change our situations in the twinkling of an eye.

He demands praise and worship from us at all times; the angels in heaven do not cease to praise Him. If we must enjoy the kingdom of God here on earth we must do as IT IS DON IN HEAVEN – Ceaselessly praise Him

As a Man Thinketh ... So Is He!

Bible Passages: Proverbs 23; Psalm 3; Jeremiah 29; Philippians 4

Proverbs 23: 6-7
...7 For as he thinketh in his heart, so is he: Eat and drink, saith he to thee...

- God's thoughts like His are different from ours. They are as far as the East is to the West! They are beyond our imagination His is limitless and infinite while we are limited and finite.
- God expects us to align our thoughts with His, by first purging ourselves from everything that is of flesh. We can only touch God by faith in the Spirit through His Son Jesus, for God is Spirit. Jesus is the only way to God who is the Father to all that believe and redeemed from the cause of the law.

The letter to the Philippians was written to believers, and Paul admonishes them (us) in to think on the things that are of good report.

- Our lives are shaped by thoughts; God's, man's including those of others. Whatever we desire to do first gets processed in our hearts.

We have thoughts for ourselves and others have for us.
- We cannot change God's thoughts for; for He including His thoughts, do not change. Likewise His purpose and will for us are eternally settled and good. There is a sure and expected end for all depending on how we handle Him, His Word and grace. We cannot determine what others think about us, but we can prevent the impact of their thoughts on our lives.
- We are to think good thoughts (ponder on the word of God), thereby warding off evil thoughts.

<u>Prayer Point:</u>

Pure thoughts and to conform to God's plan for my life

JOSHUA – A TYPE OF JESUS CHRIST

Here are some Prophecies and Symbols of Joshua fulfilled in Christ and His Church

The Names Joshua and Jesus: Joshua and Jesus are really the same name. Both from the Hebrew Yehoshua or Yeshua, in Greek Joshua, in English Jesus, which means, *"he will save"*. Joshua will provide a temporal salvation and Jesus an eternal one,

The New Testament says that Mary would bring forth a son ...*and call his name Jesus, for he shall save his people from their sins* – Matthew 1:21. The meaning is the same for both: "the LORD saves" (or "the LORD is salvation"). This etymological rendering is completely consistent with what the angel who announces Jesus' coming birth tells Joseph

The original name was Hosea ("saves"), which is also Joshua: Moses changed it into Joshua ("God's salvation"), and it was significant of the services he was to render, and typified those of a greater Savior, Jesus – Hebrews 1: 8, Numbers 13: 8.
- Jesus did the same with Peter, from Simon (soft), into Peter (rock), *And I tell you that you are Peter (Rock), and on this rock I will build my church* – Matthew 16:16.

The name "Jesus": Whether it is Yahushuah, Yahshua, Y'Shuah, and Yeshua is above all names - yet almost all the Christian and non Christian world call Him Jesus. Could you please tell me the correct history of Jesus' Greek name and what it really is in Hebrew?

Christ's given name, Jesus, means the LORD saves or the LORD is salvation. It is a Hebrew name which has been transliterated into Greek as *Iesous*.

The name of Moses' successor in the KJV is "Jesus", not "Joshua", their names are indeed identical in Hebrew and also in Greek; - Hebrews 4: 8; where it is only the context that tells the Greek reader that we are talking about Joshua and not Jesus. Most English version now translates them as if they were spelled differently.

The Hebrew name is *Yehoshu'ah* also occurs in a shortened alternative form, not an uncommon thing for Hebrew names, *Yeshu'ah*). Both forms are rendered in the Septuagint by the same Greek name, *Iesous* (the same spelling as discussed above) The New Testament takes many of its spelling conventions from the Septuagint.

Both the longer and shorter Hebrew forms are derived from two roots, being a compilation of the poetically shortened version of the divine name (*Yah* instead of *YHVH*) and the verb "to save" (*yash'ah*).

The fact that Joshua's name is really identical to that of Jesus is not a coincidence, but reflects the fact that Joshua is a type of Christ. Joshua led the people into the land, just as Jesus leads us into the holy of holies by His blood, giving us an eternal inheritance as Joshua gave a temporal one.

There are also many parallels between the coming in to the Promised Land and the second Advent and restoration of Israel Jesus is the ultimate Joshua, hence Joshua a type of the coming Messiah. Jesus has indeed saved us from our sins through His blood, and will indeed return for us to deliver us into the incalculable riches of eternity.

We can be assured not only of our deliverance *from* the devil's world and *from* this body of sin in which we now abide, but also our deliverance *into* an eternal inheritance (that puts the best of this present world to shame).

The Roles of Joshua and Jesus: Leaders of Israel

- Joshua: Moses spoke concerning Joshua – *Because of you the Lord became angry with me also and said You shall not enter it, either. But your assistant, Joshua son of Nun, will enter it. Encourage him, because he will lead Israel to inherit it* – Deuteronomy 1:37-38.
- Jesus: *"'But you, Bethlehem, in the land of Judah, are by no means least among the rulers of Judah; for out of you will come a ruler who will be the shepherd of my people Israel* – Matthew 2: 6.

Appointed by God

Joshua was appointed by God; his mission not inherited.
Jesus was appointed by God, His mission not inherited.
Both Joshua and Jesus appointed twelve men
- Joshua appointed twelve men, one from each tribe, Joshua 4:4,
- Jesus appointed twelve men as His close disciples - Mark 3: 16-19.

Unfinished Work:

In Joshua 13, Joshua did not accomplish all the work that was to be done; but left a remnant for those who came after him. Jesus left His Church to finish His Work,

He said to them, *Go into all the world and preach the good news to all creation* – Mark 16:15.

Branch: A Title of both, Joshua and Jesus:

Joshua: *"Take the silver and gold and make a crown, and set it on the head of the high priest, Joshua son of Jehozadak.* Zechariah 6:11-13.

- Jesus: *The days are coming, declares the Lord, "when I will raise up to David a righteous BRANCH.* – Jeremiah 23: 5-6.

Joshua brought the faithful to the temporal Promised Land. He killed all the gentiles defeated in the "War of Extermination"

Jesus has an eternal mission: Brings the faithful to everlasting Heaven, sends the unfaithful to eternal Hell - Matthew 25: 31-46.

- In the New Testament, Jesus fulfilled Joshua, from a temporal salvation into an eternal salvation, changed the whole attitude:
- Wars... Joshua... Jesus: Joshua is the book of the War of God; fought by men, with a "war of extermination" killing all defeated gentiles... the Old Testament will follow the same pattern...
- The answer to any war will be to turn the other cheek, because vengeance is the LORD's - Matthew .5: 39, 26:52, Romans 12: 19.
- The War of a Christian: The war of Joshua was a temporal one, to conquer the Promised Land. The war of a Christian is an eternal one – the battle of faith – to conquer the eternal Promised Land, Heaven! – 1 Timothy 6; 2 Timothy 4.
- The Weapons: For Joshua, it was the Lord, for the Lord your God will be with you wherever you go, Joshua 1: 7-9
- For the Christian, it is the same Lord; *And surely I am with you always, to the very end of the age-* Matthew 28: 20.

- The Walls of Jericho... the Sun stops: Joshua encountered difficult and even impossible tasks: The Jordan River, the Walls of Jericho. He trusted God, and God did it for him!
- A Christian will encounter also walls like Jericho, but with faith in Jesus, he will demolish them, and pass the river Jordan, and even the sun and the moon will stop, if that's what is needed – Joshua 3, 6, 10).
- The territory assigned to the Tribes – Joshua 12 to 24: In Joshua, each Tribe and each person had his own territory to take good care off.
- In Christianity, every person has also his own territory to take good care off: Help the relatives to go to Heaven, and the neighbors, and the friends and enemies... by praying for and preaching to them

For Every Christian: Renewal of the Covenant of Shechem - Joshua 24: 15-18. We too will serve the Lord, because He is our God.

WEEKS 27-39

WEEK 27

WHATSOEVER THINGS ARE OF GOOD REPORT

Bible Passages: Philippians 4; Colossians 3; 2 Corinthians 5; 1 John 3

Philippians 4: 8-11

8 Finally, brethren, whatsoever things are true, whatsoever things are honest, whatsoever things are just, whatsoever things are pure, whatsoever things are lovely, whatsoever things are of good report; if there be any virtue, and if there be any praise, think on these things...

In the King James Version of the Bible the word WHATSOEVER appears 139 times, in the Old and New Testaments. For everything we do on earth there is a record kept, and the Bible says that every secret word or act shall be made public.

We can even confirm this because God Word says that He rewards in public what we do in secret – Matthew 6: 4 - *That thine alms may be in secret: and thy Father, which seeth in secret himself, shall reward thee openly.*

God expects us to think on; consider or weigh our actions whether in private or in public, that is to always judge our actions and words to be sure that they are according to God's principles and desires for everyone. All our actions and/or inaction are open before God.

The Bible demands that we be sure our actions are right before God judged all, so that we would not be judged – 1 Corinthians 4: 5. God knows we are imperfect and face constant opposition from the devil and our flesh. Therefore in order to do right, with the help of the Holy Spirit we must know right from wrong.

This can be done by:

- Searching through the Scriptures;
- Listening to the Holy Spirit who also teaches us
- Through others – friends, neighbors, spiritual leaders, acquaintances.
- Through other channels and media; books, radio, television and internet.
- Making sure that what we hear, see or feel is mixed with faith in order to be profitable; for without faith it is not possible to please God; no doubter will receive anything from God.

This implies that we must be careful what we listen to and who we get acquainted with. This is because we are influenced by the environment we find ourselves, even we are determined to stay right, it get more difficult when we are with the wrong company;

That is those who do not fear the LORD; *the fear of the LORD is the beginning of wisdom; and the fool says in his heart there is no God...!*

After salvation, we are still here on earth. We interact with all kinds of people and deal with various issues which involve putting the Word of God into use on a daily and consistent basis.

The Word of God is alive and powerful; accomplishing everything for which God purposes it, irrespective of our position.

Our position/faith in Him determines how we prosper thereby. So we have to:

- Choose, and determined to do right, recognizing that of our own we cannot choose nor do right – as explained by Paul in Romans 8. Proverbs 25: 7; shows that as we think so are we. Ephesians 3: 20– so the starting point for God to work for, in and through us is our thoughts.
- Renew our minds; by pray without ceasing knowing that we cannot receive without asking. Also, we show our dependency and trust in God. So it does not matter whether we are new Christians or have known God all our lives, we have so much to learn of Him. He is the NEVER CHANGING GOD; His ways are past finding, His thoughts far from ours.
- Know that for a sincere seeker of the Truth, the more one knows about Him the more one find out there yet to be known. This because He chooses when, how here and what to reveal, of Himself to us! OUR RESPONSIBILITY IS TO THINK ON AND ABIDE IN HIM!

In conclusion our conduct must be in alignment with the Word of God, for we may be the first or the only Bible some people will ever read! We are the AMBASSADORS FOR CHRIST for we belong to the kingdom of God though we live here on earth!

Prayer Points:

To be taught and led by the Holy Spirit

WEEK 28

IN THE NAME OF JESUS:

The Power of Attorney

Bible Passages: John 14; 16:24-26; Matthew 7:7; Luke 18: 1-8

Jesus gave us the authority to use His name to plead our cause and obtain our desires from God, for as long as we abide in Him, just like He abides in the Father. His instructions are simple to follow:

- Ask in the name of Jesus in order to receive In addition to this Jesus expects us to SEEK, and KNOCK. He wants us to be a part of the process of obtaining from God; we are expected to participate, by trusting God, for His mercies which are new every day. Like the Manna in the desert, yesterday trust will not work for the need of today.
- We must persevere, like the widow in Luke 18: 5-8, that persistently pleaded her cause with the earthly unjust judge. With the Just God, who is our Father, who can like rivers of water turn the heart of kings, it wherever He pleases? Before Him, we the inhabitants of the earth are like grasshoppers, we are certain of receiving a just reward.
- We have the name of Jesus – the name that is above every other name, the name at which every knee must bow to present our cases before our Father and Judge.
- Most importantly we have assurance that it Jesus is the only name that God recognizes

He is our Advocate with God – 1 John 2: 1-3. He is the propitiation for our sins; His blood is eternally presented before our Father justifying us, even when the Devil the accuser of the brethren accuses us before Him of our shortcomings and failures.

So whatsoever we ask in the name of Jesus we are certain and confident that God will give us. Have you asked Him to come to your life? He does not turn any one back, rather as many as believe Him to them gave He power to be called the sons of God. So ask and you will be saved.

God Does Not Change

Bible Passages: Malachi 3; Hebrews 13: 8; Mark 5 1-20; John 4

> Malachi 3: 6 *For I am the LORD, I change not; therefore ye sons of Jacob are not consumed.*
>
> Hebrews 13: 8 *Jesus Christ the same yesterday, and today, and forever.*

One of the attributes of God is that He is immutable and unchanging. That is He cannot be moved, and is eternally the same Through the Scriptures we see that God wants us to know Him; His love and will for humanity.

He wants us to know and experience His power majesty and glory here on earth.

God is absolutely and simply a Spirit, not subject to those mutations which are found in corporate bodily nature. He is self existent, no particle or composition and not subject to changes in created spirits. From Exodus 3: 14, we know among other things God:
- Does not improve, get worse; increase, nor decrease – 1 Timothy 6: 16
- Does not die nor deteriorate, has no origin, duplicate or copy! He has no beginning nor end
- He has no new knowledge; His understanding comprehends all things, past, present and future. His love, grace, mercy and standards are constant
- His power to save, deliver and keep is never changing; His measurements; the same irrespective of creed, culture or generation.
- It is not just that He has no beginning, but does not have an end – which means we cannot expect a cessation or an end to His reign, authority or availability to make the necessary changes to our lives. We are constantly in need of change, because our lives and circumstance are affected by an innate capacity to wax old.
- The question we must answer is – "Am I willing to allow the Holy Spirit to have rule over my life?" Consider the life of John the Baptist John 1-3
- We know He does –noticeable changes occurred in the lives of the man with the legion – Mark 5: 1-20; the Samaritan woman by the well – John 4: 4-20, as they encountered Jesus. He can change us today if you will allow Him.

Prayer Point:

To understand the nature and character of God

WEEK 29

BETTER TO LIGHT A CANDLE

Bible Passages: Joshua 1; Ecclesiastes 7; Philippians 3; Hebrews 12

> Ecclesiastes 7: 1-8
> *1 A good name is better than precious ointment; and the day of death than the day of one's birth...*
> *5 It is better to hear the rebuke of the wise, than for a man to hear the song of fools....*
> *8 Better is the end of a thing than the beginning thereof: and the patient in spirit is better than the proud in spirit*

How many times we have lamented over missed/lost opportunities, failures or lack of resources to carry out or complete our plans and fulfill some set objectives in life? Let us see some Scriptures to see where God wants us to put our focus as we journey through life

- The account of Jesus concerning facing the cross – He kept His eyes on the purpose of the cross that is the goal rather than the process. Hebrews 12: 2 *Looking unto Jesus the author and finisher of our faith; who for the joy that was set before him endured the cross...*
- From Paul's writing in Philippians 3: 13-14, we can deduce that the past could be horrible, and the present challenging and probably everything, but what the Word of God says.
- As long as the earth remains, seed time and harvest time will not change, nor God's covenant of the sun and moon fail! The covenant of salt is also sure. The grace of God is eternal and unchanging, likewise His love towards us.

- Our responsibility is to obey His word that tells us to act on His Word rather than bemoan the circumstances of our lives. Also let us glory only in the fact that we know Him, not on our achievements, which are only attainable however only through His grace.
- Proverbs in 7: 8-10,... *8 Better is the end of a thing than the beginning thereof: and the patient in spirit is better than the proud in spirit* Let us keep our focus on the finished work of Christ at Calvary and the goal that He sets before us both in the immediate and the eternal future as we face each challenge of life! Thereby we make our way prosper as God purposes – Joshua 1:7

It Is Better To......

Have a good name than precious ointment: As unsatisfactory as all sublunary things are, yet there are some which are of great consequences and among them a good name.

- We know a person not just by the natural name but the name that is acquired or achieved as a result of a person's character or accomplishments.
- See the end of a thing than the beginning: Let us run the race that is set before us with patience. His ways though now in clouds and darkness to the human perception, will soon have the mist cleared from our eyes, and all the dark alleys that we have to go through will lead to the glorious end prepared for those who endure to the end. Let's not spend precious times asking why God does things rather let's learn submission to His will.

- We see in the Scriptures when God chooses to bless a person He first reveals Himself to that person by that name; for example: *Jehovah Shalom, Jehovah Jireh et c.* Then when necessary, He changes the name of the person He wants to bless to reflect the blessing at hand
- To go to a house of mourning than a house of easting: In the house of mourning there is a soberness that comes to the heart of man. There is a realization that misfortune knows no boundaries. Many times they cannot be helped but endured though drawing on the strength of God. From the house of morning we find occasion for serious and deeply edifying thoughts and reflections.
- To sorrow than to laugh: By the sorrow of the countenance, the grief of heart shows itself in the countenance. In such cases, most people try themselves at the tribunal of their own consciences, and resolve on amendment of life. In the midst of sorrow there is opportunity to reflect on the issues of life and see the sovereignty of God.
- Laughter comes from a merry heart which could be a result of drinking alcohol; but joy comes from the indwelling of the Holy Spirit. God wants us to look up to Him who is the source of our joy, for both laughter and sorrow are subject to the issues of life, but joy is the fruit of the Spirit.

<u>Prayer Points:</u>

To always portray the image of God

WEEK 30

FAITH IS, THE EVIDENCE OF...

Bible Passages: Romans 8; 1 Corinthians 13; Hebrews 11

Romans 8: 24-25

...: for what a man seeth, why doth he yet hope for?
25 But if we hope for that we see not, then do we with patience wait for it.

Some of the dictionary definitions of EVIDENCE are:
- That which tends to prove something, or a witness;
- To indicate clearly; exemplify or prove.
- To support by testimony; a ground for belief; something that furnishes or tends to furnish proof.

- Enoch, had no Pastor nor Sunday School teacher to teach him how to walk with God; he must have known that life goes beyond the physical, that is what we can see with our natural eyes, for him to choose to follow the path of righteousness.
- Prior to Noah's building of the Ark in obedience to God's instructions, there had been no rain on the earth. God's Word was simple beyond any human imagination. He had to just obey this sure Word to avoid the coming unimaginable and unstoppable catastrophe!
- Remember that; as God chose to wipe out humanity because of sin, but desirous of keeping a remnant, He called Noah to build Ark to preserve the human race.

- Since faith is the evidence of things not seen, then faith is the material proof, or that which testifies to the reality of what we hope for a desired end.

  1. The question to each believer then is: What do you hope for? Faith will validate or testify to that which we hope for. It is the surety for our hope.
  2. If there is anything wrong, it must be in: what we hope for; the evidence we present – the faith we apply. Whom we have faith in; who is in charge of the affairs of our lives

God and His Word are one and the same; they endure forever, moreover faith, hope and love abide – 1 Corinthians 13: 13 – We must apply faith in love for our God is love and hope in love that is hope in God – that is no matter our immediate need, God (Love) must be our ultimate goal. We must start and end the journey in Him and through Him.
- Jesus Christ is the Author and Finisher of our faith – Hebrews 12: 2;; He is the beginning and the concluding
- Evidence of our hope in God! Christ Jesus is and must be our hope, for He saved us from sin and death. He is the One who was made a curse for us, so that we will be free from the curse incurred from Adam and Eve. Notice this comment from Matthew 13: 58 *And he did not many mighty works there because of their unbelief.*

- It is very important; and it is to our advantage to have faith in God and His Son Jesus Christ if we are truly desirous of changes in our lives. It is only through faith in Him that we can receive a good report like the heroes and heroines listed in the Bible's Hall of faith – Hebrews Chapter 11.
- Only through faith can we draw the attention of God to our situations and lives. Not that He does not see, or know what we are going through, but that He is Just in ALL His ways, and does not break His law, to please or show that He loves us.
- When the human race was building the tower God said for as long they were united in their intents and purposes they could not be stopped. He chose to confuse the human language – Genesis 11, to stop them because their intentions were wrong.

So with good intentions and in agreement with the Word of God which is our witness for the goal set, in unity with fellow believers we are set up for greatness.

Faith works in love and with humility; a heart full of praise and a soul that worships. Our attitude of worship is a reflection of our admission of and submission to the almightiness of God who is able to DO ALL THINGS; for with Him ALL THINGS ARE POSSIBLE.

Prayer Point:

To humbly and unconditionally trust God

WEEK 31

FAITH IS, THE SUBSTANCE OF...

Bible Passages: Joshua 10: 12-14; Isaiah 37; Romans 9: 14-16.

Romans 9: 15-16
...16 So then it is not of him that willeth, nor of him that runneth, but of God that sheweth mercy.

When Job was to be restored he had to forgive and bless his persecutors, then God would move in on his behalf. Forgiveness is a relevant tool to operate in faith. God is Just. So we need to ask – What is it that we have to do to for God to be pleased with us? – Hebrews 11: 6, *without faith it is impossible to please God...*

There is a need to do a personal check on the application of our faith in order to receive the promises of God – note that we do not need to have faith for what we can see; otherwise it will be applying faith erroneously. Having faith does not imply obtaining an instant gratification or supply of need.

It only means that whether the need is met or not, our trust in the God who is able to do all things, can affect the changes whenever and however He chooses to without breaking His own laws.

The time of manifestation of promise is at the prerogative of God who determines who is to be a Moses and who to be a Pharaoh to the glory of His name.

This is because He knows what our choices will be as we mature enough to be able to choose right from wrong – Romans 9: 14-16. Sometimes God transcends natural laws, like making
- The sun dial to go backwards as a sign to Hezekiah that he will recover from his illness and live for 15 more years – Isaiah 37.
- The sun and the moon, to stand still for Joshua and the army of Israel to have light to win the war against the Amorites – Joshua 10: 12-14.
- The river Jordan to cut off, for Israel to cross over to the Promised Land – Joshua 4: 1-24.
- Lack of faith cannot stop God; He is Omnipotent. It implies that the person in need of His intervention will not be able to enjoy the miraculous.

Faith Comes By Hearing God's Word

Bible Passages: Romans 10: 1-21; Hebrews 11: 1-12; John 1

Romans 10:*17 So then faith cometh by hearing, and hearing by the word of God*
Hebrews *11:6 But without faith it is impossible to please him:*

From the Word of God we know that our journey or walk with God starts with hearing Him Speak to us. Examples – Noah, Abraham, Jacob, Moses, Joshua, Samuel and Gideon. We are to obediently act on His Word by faith.

No one have seen the Father, but He chose to manifest Himself to us in His only Begotten Son Jesus; who is the way the truth and the life. Through Jesus we have access the Father; hence all our prayers to God must be in His name – God has given Him a name that is above every name that at the mention of His name every tongue must confess and every knee bow.

In order to hear the word of God, we must understand first that He desires communication and fellowship with us individually. Jesus came for each and every one of us.

- He takes us aside like in the cases of: Moses with the burning bush when he obtained the commission to lead the children of Israel out of Egypt; and when He got the Ten Commandments.
- Joshua was aside by himself when he got instructions as to how to enter the Promised Land.
- Gideon was alone at the threshing floor as he received commission to deliver the children of Israel from the Midianites – Judges 6.
- Zachariah was alone when he was informed of the gift of a child – John the Baptist in his old age – Luke Chapter One
- Mary was alone when she got the Good News of becoming the mother of our Savior Jesus Christ.

It is as we study His Word privately or with other Believers – *Study to shew thyself worthy...* By listening to someone preach the Word, give godly instructions or counsel as to what we need to do.

<u>Prayer Point</u>: Power to hear God when He speaks to me

WEEK 32

THE ADDITIVES OF FAITH!

📖 Bible Passages: 2 Peter 1; Hebrews 11; Daniel 5

2 Peter 1:4-10

... 5 And beside this, giving all diligence, add to your faith virtue; and to virtue knowledge...

One of the purposes for which God created us, is that we FRUITFUL & MULTIPLY! God spoke the universe and all that is in it by faith, for the things which are were brought forth out that do not appear. He made us in His image – both male and female – and Jesus told us that greater works than He did shall we also do for as long as we remain/abide in Him
- God expects us to live, bear fruit, and do everything by faith. We are created in His image so if we must achieve anything it must be by the same way He did and does things. However faith without works, can take us nowhere in our walk with God and our relationship with other mortals.
- For our faith to be effective God expects us to have these virtues, in spiritual and those things that relate to the physical activities of our lives.
    - Diligence and Virtue
    - Temperance, Self control and Knowledge
    - Brotherly kindness, Sowing and Reaping
    - Love and Patience

It appears that the fruit of the Spirit must be evident in our lives for faith to be functional. For all these additives except diligence and knowledge are included in the fruit of the Spirit. Faith works on God's terms. We are to submit to His will and desire for our lives – James 4: 7.

God is a God of order; we must follow His instructions in the order for which it is presented for His Word to work for us. He demands FULL AND COMPLETE obedience from us in order for us to enjoy the promises, benefits, and the privileges of His Kingdom. He is also a God of principles; there are conditions that must be met in order to key into His plan for prosperity and success.

Time to Sow and Reap

Bible Passages: Genesis 8; Ecclesiastes 3; Luke 6; Galatians 6

Genesis 8: 22 *While the earth remaineth, seedtime and harvest, and cold and heat, and summer and winter, and day and night shall not cease.*

Man may make promises that he cannot or will not fulfill, but our God the *Jehovah Nissi;* fulfills all the promises He makes to us, including those. He made to our ancestors. His covenant to all humanity as spoken to Abraham and reestablished with Noah is that for as long as the earth remains, a season/time of harvest will follow a season/time of sowing. Jesus speaks to us through in His Word to the disciples that we are to bear fruit

He goes further to explain to sow on the good soil, and abide in Him, in order to bear fruit in abundance. The way by which we demonstrate our faith in God is in abiding in and obeying His Word. That is the way to bear fruit. In other word, Our obedience is like a seed sown which will for as long as the earth remains bear fruit! God wants us to follow is to take the seed (the Word of God); sow it; maintain and tender the crop, nurturing.

We are to diligently sow the seed of the love and compassion of God; He encourages us not to be weary or tired, as we face the many discouraging situations and circumstances along the way. We are to keep our focus on the goal that t is ahead for us. Note the following. The LORD of the harvest providentially makes the plant to bring forth fruit at the appointed time.

Prayer Points: Help to sow diligently and bountifully.

WEEK 33

SOME TRUST IN CHARIOTS AND HORSES

Bible Passages: Psalm 20; 49:6; Isaiah 31:1; 50; Acts 2

It is evident that by the natural instinct of man is to be able to lord it over other beings. This is basically the way God created us – to be fruitful, multiply, replenish and subdue the earth. So we see in the human history, the building of cities, and nations; the conquering and subjugation of kingdoms and fellow humans.

In order to prevail over opposing tribes, cities, nations and kingdoms the necessity to build arsenals and weapons came about and the developed of these progressed. As the kingdoms prevailed over one another the tendency to rely on them increased, such that the rulers of the various nations began to measure their greatness by the largeness or sophistication of their weapons.

Sometimes too wealth, affluence and prosperity are used as instruments of intimidation, oppression and conquest. We are to understand that we do not war against flesh and blood, but against spirits, powers and spiritual wickedness in high places – Ephesians 1: 20. Our weapons are not carnal but mighty through God to the pulling down of strongholds, casting down imaginations...– 2 Corinthians 10: 2-5.

The Bible tells us that whosoever shall call on the name of the Lord shall be saved. From Romans 10: 14, we know that we can only call on whom we know (hear/learn about) and trust that is believe. But putting our trust in Him, we are acknowledging that those physical weapons will do us no good outside the grace, mercy and love of God. For it is of the Lord's mercy that we are not consumed; His mercies are new every day.

Primarily we must understand that we cannot save, nor keep ourselves; so we must allow God who is able to save to the uttermost to keep, protect us and fight our battles for us. So like Paul let us trust God to be Lord over our lives such that we will be able to confess that let our boast be in that we know God

The Name of the LORD is a Strong Tower

Bible Passages: Proverbs 18: 14-20; Isaiah 50: 10

Proverbs 18: 10-11
10 The name of the LORD is a strong tower: the righteous runneth into it, and is safe.
11 The rich man's wealth is his strong city, and as an high wall in his own conceit.

The name of the LORD is to the righteous what:
- Wealth is to the rich;
- Armory/Weaponry is to the warrior;
- Position is to the great;
- A city or nation is to the king or ruler

These different categories of people and achievers, if unbelievers trust in the things they possess, but the believer is admonishes to have a change of heart.

It is only those who put their trust in the name of the LORD which is a strong tower that will be saved/protected/kept. We are saved; kept and win battles by grace; hence:
- Ahab the king of Israel sent to Benhadad king of Syria in 1 Kings 20: 11 *And the king of Israel answered and said, Tell him, Let not him that girdeth on his harness boast himself as he that putteth it off.*
- And Paul wrote to the Romans 9: 16
- The seventy disciples returned testifying that the devils were subject to the devils were subject to the in the name of Jesus – Luke 10: 17.
- The multitude followed Jesus crying *Hosanna* hailing Him as he rode on an ass to Jerusalem, honoring Him for coming in the name of the LORD – Mark 11: 9.
- Peter at Pentecost reiterates God's promise – Acts 2: 21 ... *that whosoever shall call on the name of the Lord shall be saved.*

So we must acknowledge Jesus who has been given a name that is above every name. At the mention of His name by faith, we are kept in the will of God. And for as long as we are kept in God's will we able to thrive and accomplish all that He purposed for us.

Prayer Point: Grant O LORD that I will know You and the power of the resurrection.

WEEK 34

THE NAMES OF GOD – *The Jehovah Rophi*

Bible Passages: Exodus 15: 22-27; 3 John

Exodus 15: 22-27
22 So Moses brought Israel from the Red sea, and they went out into the wilderness of Shur; and they went three days in the wilderness, and found no water...

The LORD has always given His people ever-increasing revelations of His character. He does not just proclaim His name or who He is, but leads us to discover Him. God wants us to know His character and nature. In Romans 10: 17, Paul states: - *Faith cometh by hearing and hearing by the word of God...*

It is the word that reveals who God is to us; that produces the faith necessary to receive from Him. We must discover Him, by seeing and believing for ourselves who He claims to be! We believe by faith but know Him by the demonstration of His power and character (through His actions)! Read the encounter of the Israelites at Marah – Exodus 15: 22-27.

Immediately after the miraculous deliverance of the Israelites from the Red Sea, they came to a place called Marah, thirty and exhausted. Within days they had progressed from the heights of praise to the depths of despair!

Thirsty and tired the only water available was too bitter to drink, nor quench their thirst!

Have you ever been in this kind of situation? Or rather maybe you are facing such now. You are not alone, it does not matter how, when or where the bitterness came into our lives, He wants to heal us, spirit soul and body –

Just as God took these Israelites to a point where Moses had to cry to the LORD for healing of the water. God allows some encounters in our lives to prove Himself as our *Jehovah Rophi,* if we cry for help.

He is our Healer and will heal you, only if you call upon Him. In summary in the process of experiencing God as our *Jehovah Rophi,* we must: -

- Identify and acknowledge the bitterness in our lives
- Realize that we cannot change the bitterness on our own
- Seek help from God – sometimes through a Spiritual Leader/another Christian
- Together we must call on God for help; He never fails. We will discover that He is able and ready to heal us, spirit, soul and body!

He Who Dwells In The Secret Place...

Bible Passages: Psalm 91; 2 Peter 3:8

God expects and demands continual, constant and consistent fellowship with us. We cannot overemphasize the need to dwell in His presence at all times. We know that in His presence there is fullness of joy and at His right hand pleasures forever.
Do you desire fullness of joy?
Do you wish to be kept by His everlasting arms?
Do you intent to be at the right place at the right time for the right purpose?

If your answers to these questions are yes then you need to pay a closer attention to His Word. As God's children we must understand that He is the One who draws us to Himself, when we draw close to Him. Although He is the initiator, His initiation is not imposed on our will. He allows us to choose.

When we draw nigh to Him, that is separate ourselves from worldly lusts and behaviors, He pulls us to Him by His grace, and overshadows us such that the sun that is the evil of the day, does not smite us by day nor the moon by night. Peter says in 2 Peter 3: 8

Spending eternity with Him is a thing to be desired, but we can enjoy His presence right here by dwelling in His secret place as we praise, worship and seek His face in the place of prayer daily and consistently. When the righteous run into His name they are:
- Delivered from curses, diseases, sicknesses, poverty; sin and death;
- Kept from sin and allow Him to have rule over them

Prayer Points: To know that Christ Jesus is the source of my faith

WEEK 35

PRAYER CHANGES THINGS

Bible Passages: Luke 18; Matthew 17: 14; Galatians 6: 9

Matthew 17: *21 Howbeit this kind goeth not out but by prayer and fasting.*

The Bible reports that Jesus prayed continually at every stage of His life and ministry. Great deliverances and manifestations of the power of God were wrought as they sought God by prayers and supplication.

The disciples seeing the prayer life of Jesus asked Him to teach them how to pray; they must have seen the effectiveness of His prayers. The Old Testament also shows us how the patriarchs prayed when they were in difficult and undesired situations.

In each case reported we see God responding to the prayers of His people by showing in various ways with answers to their requests. A few examples are; there are many more examples:
- Abraham prayed for a child
- The people of Israel prayed for deliverance from the oppression of Egypt
- Jabez prayed for a prosperity;
- Hannah prayed for a son.
- Job called to be healed and restored

- David prayed for repentance and restoration of the Holy Spirit – Psalm 51.
- Nehemiah prayed for favor to go rebuild the wall at Jerusalem – Nehemiah 2.
- Esther and all Israel prayed for favor from the king and for deliverance from the slaughter initiated by Haman – Esther 7-10.
- Daniel prayed for deliverance from lions when he was thrown into their den; and for the deliverance of Israel from Babylonian enslavement – Daniel 4; 9
- The New Testament Christians chose the replacement to Judas by prayers – Acts 1: 24.
- Their great encounter with the Holy Spirit as they assembled together in one accord, though prayers was not specifically mention, we know they prayed; because elsewhere we see them pray as they gathered together as their manner was – Acts 2
- They prayed for the release of Peter – Acts 8: 15.

Let My People Go...

Bible Passages: Exodus 5-9; 1 Peter 1

Exodus 5: 9 *And the LORD spake unto Moses, Go unto Pharaoh, and say unto him, Thus saith the LORD, Let my people go, that they may serve me.*
God created us for worship and fellowship, but at the fall of man we lost all that privilege. Christ Jesus however came to set us free and as many as believe Him to them gave He power to be called the sons of God.

Being a child of God assures privileges and commands responsibilities from every believer. After God saved us He would have taken us to heaven, but He wants us to establish His kingdom here on earth. He saved us so that we can continue to declare His Word here to all; for the gospel must be preached to all the nooks and corners of the earth and to all men, before the end comes.

Everyone must hear that JESUS SAVES and that God wants us to serve Him. We each must be willing to tell Pharaoh (a type of Satan) to release God's people so that they may serve God. Jesus was manifested to destroy the works of the devil, and to reconcile all that come to Him with the Father.

The responsibility is laid on us to speak on the behalf of the people (all peoples) whom Christ died and was raised for; it is the responsibility of all that hear to receive; while it is the prerogative of God to save all that He has predestinated to be saved. Remember that only the first born of the Israelite in houses of the Israelites were kept from the destroyer – Exodus 12: 23; 1Peter 1.

According to God's order we are to resist the devil, that is confront him with the word of God. Let us choose to serve the LORD, diligently and consistent. As we do that we can boldly declare resist the devil, and we can accomplish God's plans and purposes.

Prayer Point:

For the spirit of intercession

WEEK 36

OF DOORS AND GATES

📖 Bible Passages: 2 Samuel 3; Isaiah 45; Matthew 16; John 10; Revelation 3.

Matthew 16: 18 *And I say also unto thee, That thou art Peter, and upon this rock I will build my church; and the gates of hell shall not prevail against it*

Doors moved on pivots of wood fastened in sockets above and/or below - Proverbs 26:14. They were fastened by a lock Judges 3:23, 25; Song of Solomon 5:5; or a bar Judges 16:3; Job 38:10.
- The *Valley of Achor* is called a *Door of Hope*, because immediately after the execution of Achan the Lord said to Joshua, *Fear Not*, and from that time Joshua went forward in a career of uninterrupted conquest.
- Paul speaks of a door opened for the spread of the gospel - 1 Corinthians 16:9; 2 Corinthians 2:12; Colossians 4:3.
- Christ Jesus is the door that leads to all other doors – Jesus spoke of Himself in John 10: 9. He is the door that leads to all other doors. John the beloved in Revelation 4: 1 speaks of a *door opened in heaven*.
- Sometimes God opens the door of heaven to us; literally meaning door of revelation of His will, purpose, nature and character to us human beings.
- To direct the affairs of individuals, persons, peoples and generations.

We may not individually be able to control entry into and out of the gates of our cities, for this is under the supervision of the rulers of such cities.

But we have full control over those who penetrate the doors of our hearts; God shows that He will not come in if we do not open the door for Him.

Our choice concerning Him and His saving grace affects all other decisions that we will ever or have to make in life.

The responsibility rests on us to choose whom to allow into and have rule over our hearts. Whoever controls the heart has authority over the mind; and the mind ruminates over what the heart pumps into it! The choice has to be made swiftly and constantly for all the issues of our lives; where to spend eternity and enjoying the kingdom of God here on earth.

Knowing that God comes into your heart and life at your invitation, would you invite Him today? He receives all that genuine come to Him!

Gates are entrances to places – cities, palaces, tombs, camps, prisons, the Temple and its courts. They were made of:
- Iron and brass Psalm 107:16; Isaiah 45:2; Acts 12:10.
- Stones and pearls – Isaiah 54:12; Revelation 21: 21.
- Wood – Judges 16: 3.

At the gates of cities courts of justice were frequently held, and hence "judges of the gate" are spoken of in Deuteronomy 16:18; 17:8; 21:19; 25:6-7.

At the gates prophets also frequently delivered their messages – Proverbs 1:21; 8:3; Isaiah 29:21; Jeremiah 17:19, 20; 26:10). Criminals were punished without the gates – 1 Kings 21:13; Acts 7:59. By the "gates of righteousness" we are to understand those of the temple Psalm 118:19.

The gates of hell – Matthew 16:18, generally interpreted as meaning the power of Satan, but probably they may mean the power of death, denoting that the Church of Christ shall never die. So we know that gates lead to places just as doors are provided to limit or control entrance to enclosures. Sometimes we may not be able to restrain those who enter into the gates of our cities, but we have full control over those who penetrate the doors of our hearts.

When Joab took Abner aside into the middle of the gate – 2 Samuel 3: 27, to murder him, it was like taking him out to execute judgment on Abner. If Abner had been in Hebron the city of refuge and not without its gates he might have escaped the avenger's sword!

God wants to be in the City of Refuge – Christ Jesus is our City of Refuge; indeed He is our Rock like Peter states in 1Peter 2; and whoever falls on Him is broken into pieces and whomsoever He falls on is ground into powder. But when we stand on or take shelter in Him we safe and kept by His grace and power. Jesus promised to build His church on the foundation of the revelation of the truth of who He is – the MESSIAH.

The authority or power of hell will not be able to overcome the church. This should be enough for us to completely rely on Him to give us the grace and power us to stand, even in seemingly hopeless situations and circumstances.

<u>Prayer Points</u>: For Christ's full access to my heart.

WEEK 37

LET NOT THE WISE GLORY IN HIS WISDOM!

Bible Passages: Jeremiah 9: 23; Proverbs 3: 5-8

Jeremiah 9: 23 *Let not the wise msn glory in his wisdom, neither let the mighty man glory in his might, let not the rich man glory in his riches...*

Proverbs says that the glory of the young man is in his strength, while that of the old man his grey hair, which is synonymous with wisdom. This Book also tells us that wisdom is the principal thing and that with all our getting we should get, understanding as well Christ is the wisdom of God.

The Word of God instructs us to seek Christ with our minds and souls, and all the zeal and energy that He has given us. Having been reconciled to God through Christ though we must realize that He is the Only One who can draw us to Himself – It is by grace that we are saved, not based on our
- Efforts; Wisdom; Knowledge/Education
- Wealth/Resources; BY GRACE – Let us acknowledge God in all our ways. By so doing, He will direct our path – Proverbs 3: 5-8.

James admonishes us believers to ask God for wisdom, if we lack we lack it – this implies that God expects that we have wisdom.

It was GRACE that saved us and it is GRACE that will keep us! So like David we must always give God all the praise and glory, which are due Him as we live, move and have our being in Him! BE HUMBLE!

All that we have came from and belongs to Him, for in Him all things consist. So it must be borne in our minds that we must acknowledge God for every achievement and accomplishment. Actually He purposed that we bear fruit, and bearing fruit is a sign of growth and advancement; for a fruit is a sign that a living being can continue.

Seed comes from fruit it is the means by which a generation is propagated and continues. By producing fruits (seeds) we fulfill God's plan for us to replenish the earth

Therefore we must know that our fruitfulness is a fulfillment of God's word in response to our obedience and so to God must all the glory be. "One might be tempted to think or say but I worked hard to achieve so and so". Sure you worked hard but it is He who makes all grace abound to us that we having all sufficiency abounds to every good work.

Moreover do not forget that *it is not of him that wills, nor runs but of God who shows mercy* - To Him then belongs all the glory and honor.

God is No Respecter of Persons

Bible Passages: Psalm 18; Acts 10; Romans 2

Acts 10: 34-35
34 ...Peter opened his mouth and said. Of a truth I perceive that God is no respecter of persons...

Consider the effect of the positioning of the sun on the different parts of the earth: At the equator, there are twelve equal hours of daylight and darkness; and an even distribution of seasons.

On the two sides of the equator there are six to eighteen hours of daylight and darkness in the year. When the daylight is longer the weather is warmer and *vice versa.*

- The wind, sea, moon and sun all work together to affect the heat, humidity and other climatic conditions in the regions of the earth. However let us consider the fact that all these creations of God impact our lives based on our positioning with them at every particular point in time in our lives.
- These physical occurrences are pointers to spiritual ones–God is Spirit and we are too! It is therefore wise to know that we might have to change our position, in order to change some of the situations in our lives. God's position is constant like the sun – note that Jesus Christ our Savior is referred to in Malachi 4: 2,

- Just like we must find out and move to the location where the climate and weather is favorable to our well being, so must we find out God's perfect will for our lives and shift our position to be aligned to His will, if we must enjoy His blessings.

He will show respect to us by manifesting His love, goodness and mercy as we show respect to His Word and reverence the Holy Spirit, who indwells us. He honors us when we honor Him, especially when we show a willingness to conform to His image!

Prayer Points: To be diligent in every area of my life.

WEEK 38

WHO ARE YOU?

📖 Bible Passages: Psalm 139; Matthew 6; 1 Corinthians 2:10; Philippians. 3; Isaiah 51:11

This is a commonly asked question by people who are acquainted with or wish to be aquatinted with us. Many a times also we ask ourselves this same question. Let us consider the response that God expects us t give, which must come from within, and not from without for it to have any positive and God expected effect on our lives!

The Jews asked Jesus this same question, and He asked His disciples also who they and others think He was - Read Luke; John

From Hebrews 11, we know that FAITH is the distinguishing factor between those who walked right with God and those who did not. God expects us to be filled with joy and to respond to this question with confidence assured that we are truly redeemed by the blood of the Lamb.

And sanctified by His Spirit. Our response then should go thus... ... and much more based on the Word of God!
- A child of God adopted by Christ Jesus
- A royal priesthood
- A chosen generation

- A peculiar and unique person – fearfully and wonderfully made in the image of God. Each time you see me you see the image of God
- I am blessed and a blessing to my generation.
- I am righteous and as bold as the lion.
- I am the light of the world
- I am the salt of the earth
- I reign with Jesus far above principalities, powers, dominion and all that exalts itself against the knowledge of God. I am more than conqueror; neither height, depth, wealth, poverty; people or issues shall be able to separate me from His love.
- I am engraved in His palm! The list is endless but this can only be true if we are citizens of heaven – John wrote in 1 John 2: 15-17 that we must, not love nor be of the world.

This is possible, because Jesus our Prime Example led the way for us –we can do ALL THINGS THROUGH CHRIST WHO STRENGTHENS US – Philippians 4: 13

In The Image of God

Bible Passages: Read Romans; Philippians; Psalm 139: 14-15
Psalm 139:14 -15
14 I will praise thee; for I am fearfully and wonderfully made: marvellous are thy works; and that my soul knoweth right well...

We must find out God's plan and purposes for our lives; assured that God is a God of PLAN, PURPOSE AND ORDER. So our greatest requirements in life are:

- Each person must find his talent, gift, and calling within community we find ourselves
- Know that to every creature, person, family, neighborhood, city, nation, kingdom or universe, no matter how small or great God has specific plans and purposes (destiny) for each one. Each one is cut out for specific and corporate niche.
- We must be determined to listen to God through the various means He has made available to us and be willing to change directions when needed
- We must also understand that we can be fulfilled only if we choose to be WHO HE HAS MADE US TO BE! For instance Paul admonishes us that He that gives let him give liberally; one who prophesied should do so according to the proportion of his faith etc – 1 Corinthians 12: 4-12
- Surely *I can do all things through Christ who strengthens me* – Philippians 4: 13. There is a special pair of shoes that God has cut and made for each person. It is by His grace and mercy that each one can glorious wear his/her shoes!
- However, whoever we are, or whatever we become in Him, has to be in love, for love is the sure path to glory, and victory in Christ Jesus You are who Christ says you are – UNIQUE AND PRECIOUS!!!

Prayer Point: To have assurance that I am special to God, irrespective of what others think or say about me.

WEEK 39

WHAT IS SUCCESS?

Bible Passages: Joshua 1; Philippians 3:12-16; 1 Corinthians 2: 9

Joshua 1: 8 ... *thou shalt make thy way prosperous, and then thou shalt have good success.*

Philippians 3: 13-14
13 Brethren, I count not myself to have apprehended: but this one thing I do, forgetting those things which are behind, and reaching forth unto those things which are before,..

There is a constant urge and desire in all human beings to progress, advance and improve on our lots and standards; the desire to succeed. But as Christians there is need to understand godly success and achievement so that fleshly competition and rivalry will not be our lot. We must be able to define what success is and is not in order to be able to achieve success! Success is:

- Not money, nor power;
- Not goal or destiny reaching
- A journey
- The progressive achievement of God's purpose for our lives as we relate with other creatures.

- Measured by the obstacles and mountains surmounted.

Problems and failures when properly handled do transform us and work for our good in the realization of our destinies. God loves and cares for us as individuals but He is also interested in the larger picture of the salvation and redemption of the human race.

He allowed His only Begotten Son Jesus to die on the cross for us. He allows people to be martyred for the sake of the Gospel, because He knows that these ones will spend eternity with Him.

There is always a price to pay for advancement; so let's see the challenges we face as stepping stones to going higher in Christ. Let us learn to keep our focus on Christ Jesus; so that we can achieve great success. Notice that Joshua must abide in the Law/Word of God, as Jesus told us to abide in Him to bear fruit.

The Good and Perfect Employer!

Bible Passages: Matthew 20:; John 4; Revelation 22

Matthew 20: 1-20
1 For the kingdom of heaven is like unto a man that is an householder, which went out early in the morning to hire laborers into his vineyard.....

The experience of these workers with this householder, whom he hired to work in his vineyard, Jesus compares to what operates in the kingdom of heaven, is worthy of note; at this point in time in the history of the Church.

We find all through human history that God has always engaged the services of human being to carry out His divine assignments, including the coming of the Lord Jesus to earth in the form of man, using Mary His mother and Joseph to be a father to Him.

Men were used in writing the Scriptures and men and women are engaged in the spread of the Gospel today. Jesus chose, trained and worked with twelve disciples; and sent out seventy at a time – Luke 10; they were sent out with authority and power to preach the Gospel.

Some disciples who catered for Him prepared Him for burial and even provided the burial site. Just like the householder, God is still hiring and employing the services of men and women today, with promises of reward/wages.

Jesus told Peter that no one has left father and mother for the sake of the Gospel shall go unrewarded in this life and in the life to come there is life everlasting waiting for such! He is calling us to keep our focus on Him not on the other workers Let continue to pray that the God of harvest will recruit more workers to the vineyard. He comes quickly with His reward –

Prayer Points: Empowerment to be an achiever

JESUS CHRIST IN ALL HUMAN ENDEAVOR

- In Biology, He was born without the normal conception; and raised a dead man who was already decomposing; He was crucified dead and buried; yet on the third day He rose again from the dead never to die again!
- In Chemistry, He turned water to wine;
- In Economics, He disproved the law of diminishing returns by feeding over 5,000 with two fishes and five loaves of bread with twelve baskets remaining. He also fed over 4,000 with seven loaves and a few fishes, with seven baskets left.
- In Government, He never started a physical kingdom or empire but He rules in the affairs of men – for He is the reference point of every kingdom before and after Him;
- The Bible calls Him Wonderful, Counselor, Prince of Peace; and of His Kingdom there shall be no end
- In History, He is the beginning and the end; the Alpha and the Omega. He knows the end of a story before it began! In fact the word HISTORY comes from HIS STORY!
- In Medicine, He cured the sick, caused the blind to see, the lame to walk, the deaf to hear and the dumb to speak, without administering a single dose of drugs; He spoke life and health to the lives of those that asked of Him.
- In Physics, He disproved the law of gravity when He walked on water and ascended into heaven in the cloud; He will come back same way He went.
- In Religion, He said no one comes to the Father except through Him; He is the same yesterday, today and forever; He is the Way the Truth and the Life; And the Door to the Father.

Who is He? He is Jesus Christ of Nazareth. In Him all things consist both in the heavens and on earth. Behold He stands at the door of every heart, knocking and ready to enter, wine, and dine with all that will allow Him to. We are to celebrate and honor Him.
- Where do you stand with the Prince of Peace? It appointed for man once to die, after which is judgment.
- Where do you intend to spend eternity?

Your response to the call of the Messiah today will determine the answer to that question. Tomorrow may be too late – today is the day of salvation; do not harden your heart, rather humble yourself and accept Him as your Lord and Savior. He does not cast away any one that comes

Bible Passages: Matthew 24: 14; Luke 24: 44-47; John 1:12; 3:16, 36; Acts 16: 30-31; 28: 24; Romans 1: 14-18; 5: 1; 10: 9-10; 2 Corinthians 5: 20; Colossians 2: 13; Titus 3:7.

WEEKS 40-52

WEEK 40

PUTTING ON THE WHOLE ARMOR

Bible Passages: Ephesians 6; 1 Samuel 17; 2 Corinthians 10: 1-5

Ephesians 6: 10-16
10 Finally my brethren, be strong in the Lord, and in the power of his might
11 Put on the whole armor of God that ye may be able to stand against the wiles of the devil....

In the Bible passage above, we see Paul telling the Ephesians Christians, and this is applicable to us, that in order to stand right before God, we must be properly and completely dressed up in the armor of God. His message also implies that we are in constant battle with an enemy who is unrelenting in his opposition to our progress in our walk with God.

Our responsibility is to be properly armed, prepared for and willing to engage the devil in battle. James tells us to submit to God and resist the devil; while in another letter admonishes us to flee fornication (sin). There is one thing we need to keep in mind, that the devil and his cohorts have an organized and hierarchal system and are unrelentingly persistent.

So we must be in a constant state of alert and readiness to resist and establish God's kingdom everywhere we find ourselves. God demands that we put on each piece of the armor prayerfully and at all times; not just to know the word of God but: -
- To renounce the hidden things of dishonesty
- Not to walk in craftiness
- Not to handle the word of God deceitfully
- Manifest the truth, commending ourselves to every man's conscience in the sight of God.

We must recognize that the enemy is not the person hurting us, but the devil/an evil spirit, who is out not just to hurt us but to make us have wrong impressions. Thereby he cause division among us and alienates us from the people for whom Christ died.

The purpose of the devil in doing this is that once he can alienate us, then he can continue to work on our minds and thoughts and make us to denounce God, and His love for us. Therefore let us daily put on the armor of God and be prepared to confront the devil and the issues he brings rather the people God has blessed us with.

It is the evil spirit that works in people to make them want to oppose us. We are to remember that people do not come into our lives by accident; God knows about them and whatever they do will work for our good for as long as we abide in Christ Jesus.

Passing Over To The Other Side!

Bible Passages: Mark 4: 35-41;

Mark 4: 35-41
35 And the same day, when the even was come, he saith unto them, Let us pass over unto the other side....

The journey of life is filled with continual activity and passing from one location, place, position, goal, community and so on and so forth to another.

This is just a part of human nature, to search for better opportunities or new perspectives, visions, or sometimes for a specific purpose. However in moving from one point to another we are sometimes confronted with opposition and challenges from other human beings or the elements.

Remember God created the light, sun moon, stars the seas, winds, the dry land, the firmament and the spirits including the angels. Glory be to God in the highest, who gave us dominion over all the creatures that operate in the earth. He gave us authority over all His creation.

In this encounter with the forces of nature, and in the company of His disciples, Christ Jesus demonstrated that He has authority over ALL. For as long as you are God's child, Christ's promise of power over all forces that oppose our advancement to the other side stands.

This is because His word endures forever. Just as He was not perturbed by the raging sea waves and winds; He was asleep, but calmly woke up alert and available to stop the waves and sea and assure the disciples that their Master is ALWAYS ready to take them through.

Are you troubled because of the opposition to your advancement? Does appear that God is asleep on you? Do you feel alone and neglected by the God who promised

Prayer Points:
To be dressed and armed according to God's Word.

WEEK 41

DID YOU SAY SEVEN TIMES LORD?

Bible Passages: Matthew 18: 21-26

Matthew 18: 21-28
21 Then came Peter to him, and said, Lord, how oft shall my brother sin against me, and I forgive him? till seven times?
22 Jesus saith unto him, I say not unto thee, Until seven times: but, Until seventy times seven.

Like the apostle Peter so many times we are tempted to ask the Lord how much more times we have to forgive, those who offend us. It is easier to think of someone offending us than having to experience offence, especially when it is repeated over and over.

Important things to note about our walk with God:
- Obedience must be total, for with God there is no middle way, we are either for or against
- The necessity to obey must not be based on the convenience of the commandment/Word of the LORD. We know that every bit of His Word, is true and perfect, hence we must follow it irrespective of how we feel or think.
- He strengthens us by the power of the Holy Spirit - sometimes He may use people, angels, animals or events to take us through the difficult roads of life when we choose to OBEY HIM

- Our attitudes should be "If He says it, that settles it, irrespective of my feelings, comfort or discomfort"

This week therefore let us take a moment to:
- Review the events of our lives;
- Reflect on those that have hurt us and those we have hurt;
- Ask that God will help us to forgive those that we need to forgive;
- Ask those that need to forgive us to do the same;
- Ask for grace to make necessary changes if and when necessary

Therefore we must be ready and willing to forgive those who offend us as many times and seventy times seven! Remember there is no description of what kind of offence!

Jabez Knew His Necessity

Bible Passages 1 Chronicles 4: 9-10; Matthew 11: 28,

1 Chronicles 4: 9-10
9 And Jabez was more honourable than his brethren: and his mother called his name Jabez, saying, Because I bare him with sorrow....

Jabez recognized that his name testified to the fact that he was born in sorrow,

He knew that, the name reflected his problem everywhere he went, hence. He called on the LORD (The God of Israel), who can do ALL THINGS, including CHANGING HIS LIFE!

The LORD who changed the direction of the life of Jabez is available today and has promised through His Son Jesus or Redeemer and Savior that He does not cast away any one that comes to Him.

It does not matter, how or when the problem started God is able to wash us clean with the precious blood of His Son Jesus, redeem and make us whole.

He promised in Matthew 11: 28, to come with our labor, problems and issues and that He will exchange them for His light weight, which includes love, peace, joy and His blessing that makes rich and does not adds no sorrows to it.

The first step to victory and triumph is to COME TO HIM as you are and be prepared for Him to CHANGE you to who He created you to be - a reflection of His glory - He created you in His image. All through the Scriptures, we see men and women who have great and dramatic changes made to lives and those whom they care about have achieved this, through:
- Recognizing that the situation is not good enough; that there is a better option
- Recognizing that there is only One Person who can make the necessary changes to the situation and circumstances
- Humbly and by faith, running to or calling on the LORD, who is not limited by time or space.

Like Jabez, we too can have dramatic changes in every area of our lives today, if we will like all the men and women of the Scriptures, whose lives testify that God rewards all who diligently seek Him.

Prayer Points:
Dear LORD, I humbly pray that You all my crooked roads straight in the precious name Jesus

WEEK 42

THE GOLDEN ALTAR

Typical and Spiritual Significance

Bible Passages: Psalm 141: 2; John 16: 18; Revelation 5

Revelation 5: 8 *the four beasts (living creatures) and four-and-twenty elders fell down before the Lamb, having every one of them harps, and golden vials full of odors (incense), which are the prayers of saints*

The burning of incense in the holy place is regarded as an emblem of prayer. David employed it – Psalm 141: 2; John, in his vision of heaven, tells us that when he had taken the book - Revelation 5: 8. As the sweet fragrance of smoking incense is most agreeable to the senses, so are the prayers of God's children very pleasing and acceptable to Him.

The brazen altar is considered a type of Christ with respect to His atonement; the golden altar a type of Him with respect to the other part of His priestly office – His intercession. He not only bled for us on the cross, a sacrifice for our sins, He is our Advocate with the Father pleads for us before the heavenly throne.

The golden altar was before the ark or throne, the veil, however, being suspended between; but Christ, with no intervening veil, is before the throne in heaven. It was from an altar with blood-sprinkled horns that the evening and morning incense ascended. See in His pierced hands and feet the blood-sprinkled horns.

He holds up the very hands that were once nailed to the accursed tree. From before the heavenly throne He is now looking down lovingly upon all that believe in Him, inviting and encouraging them to offer up their prayers, and assuring them that He Himself will present them, and secure gracious answers by releasing rich and soul-satisfying blessings.

Have you been washed in the blood of the Lamb?

Are you born again? If yes, then listen to His encouraging voice as it comes from the golden altar — John 16: 18. The issue is not that your situation cannot change but that you must ask Him in faith to make the necessary changes.

He is never too late or too early; but always on time. If you ask today and nothing happens, ask again until something happens; truly something will happen and it is for your good.

Christ And The Cloudy Pillar – Our Guide

Bible Passages: Exodus 13: 20-24; Psalm 23; 119: 105; John 16

Christ is to the Christian pilgrim what the cloudy pillar was to the Israelites. Like the Cloudy Pillar, Christ Is a Guide:

1. Christ Guides by His Example

He says, *I am the way*. As long as we walk in the path made by His blessed footsteps we shall not lose the road to glory. Christ, like the pillar, goes before this people, and says *Follow Me*.

- When confronted with temptations, we are to place the tempter behind our back; like Him going about continually doing well. By being imitators of Jesus, we make progress in our heavenward journey.
- Christ prayed often. Before break of day He climbed the solitary mountain to have communion with His Father. Let us follow His footsteps up the mount of devotion, and we shall be refreshed with gracious blessings to our souls from Him

Christ Guides by His Word

The Bible, the written word, like the angel pillar, is an ever present and seen guide – Proverbs 6:22-23.

We can see it with our bodily eyes, feel it with our hands, open it where we may, and discern it ever pointing onward and upward.

If we follow its guidance, we will not miss the way, nor fail to reach the shores of Canaan.

3. **Christ Guides by the Holy Spirit:–** Whom He promised to send to guide us into all truth – John 16: 13. By this and other agencies Christ, our Pillar of Cloud, ever leads us in the right direction for as long as we allow Him to, even when like the cloud He may seem to be acting otherwise.

When mountains rise between us and our goals; and great deeps intervene between us and them; when the road looks like the wrong way; it is the right one after all. Like Job we must be ready to affirm that we will obey Him no matter what Job 13:15–Psalm 23:4; Daniel 4:35.

Prayer Points:

Guidance by Holy Spirit at all times.

WEEK 43

EXCEPT THE LORD BUILDS...

Bible Passages: Psalm 127; Exodus 4-14; Hosea 1; Romans 9

Psalm 127: 1-2
1 Except the LORD build the house, they labor in vain that build it: except the LORD keep the city, the watchman waketh but in vain.
2 It is vain for you to rise up early, to sit up late, to eat the bread of sorrows: for so he giveth his beloved sleep.

The word "house" may refer either to an ordinary dwelling; to the temple, as a place of worship; or to a family, with reference to its success and prosperity, as the word house is often used now. The same idea of dependence is here repeated in another form. The preservation of a city depends wholly on God, whatever care or precaution may be used.

Here the Psalmist is turning our attention the importance of relying on God for every aspect of our human endeavors. No matter our skill, strength, or profession; all will be in vain unless/except God enables and assists us in accomplishing our goals and aspirations in life.

We are dependent on Him for life, for health, for strength, for practical wisdom, for a disposition to continue our work, and for success in it. Our work is susceptible to climatic changes weather, fire, tempest, earthquake and various human attacks, of enemies; but we are entirely dependent of God for safety, protection and sustenance.

Truly, God has given us the power to achieve, and build cities and establish kingdoms including His kingdom everywhere we find ourselves here on earth.

However, we must recognize our limitations, knowing that it is with Him we can do *all things through Christ who strengthens* – Philippians 4: 13. And we are kept for as long as we dwell in the secret place of the Most High God – Psalm 91: 1-3.

As you go through the activities of today consider these questions. Your answers to them show your relationship with the Almighty God who is always awake – Psalm 121. God honors your choice, which affects the your peace
- Where do you dwell?
- Who is your Watchman
- Who is the builder of your city/dream/goal
- Who is in charge of your life?

Tabitha (Dorcas) – Full of Good Works

Bible Passages: 1 Corinthians 3; 2 Corinthians 9; Acts 9-10; 1Peter 1

Acts 9: 36-42
36 Now there was at Joppa a certain disciple named Tabitha, which by interpretation is called Dorcas: this woman was full of good works and

Christianity is about relationships, that is :
- Relationship with God
- Relationship with Believers
- Relationship with Unbelievers. They may include unsaved family members, neighbors and others in the society.

When Jesus was asked if He was truly the Messiah, by the disciples of John, He pointed them to the good works that He was doing – Luke 7:22. He also affirmed that every work that we do while in the body will be judged by God finally – Luke 13: 27-33.

The letters of the apostles to the churches are all about teaching us our responsibilities to God and all the members of the society – leaders, servants/subordinates, and friends/foes. God expects us to be holy (a people of character) love Him with all our hearts, minds and souls and love our neighbors as ourselves.

Our love must be reflected in, or demonstrated by our works – Peter told Cornelius's family that Jesus went about doing good – healing the sick and casting out devils. These relationships call for responsibilities, diligence and determination to sustain and maintain

Like Tabitha/Dorcas, God expects our love for Him and others to be reflected in the things we do. We are gifted differently but the same Spirit works in us. Our responsibility is to determine what our gifting is and to use it wisely and diligently for the Body of Christ knowing and assured that God will not forget our labor of love, if we faint not.

It is through a disciplined way of life that we can walk consistent with God and it is by a consistent walk with Him that we can please Him!

<u>Prayer Points</u>: To surrender my life totally to God

WEEK 44

WHO IS A TRUE SERVANT?

Bible Passages: Genesis 1-3; 24; Matthew 25; Luke 19; Mark 16

Genesis 24: 33-34
34 And he said, I am Abraham's servant.

We discover as we go through God's word that a person cannot do everything by him/herself, hence we see in the history of mankind, that people tend to acquire servants to help in the management of their affairs. This is after the pattern of God who purposes that mankind whom He created after His image to be involved in the affairs of propagation, replenishment and dominion of the earth.

For a person to become or qualify to be a servant – he/she must be acquired, bought (or redeemed from slavery). Sometimes some people volunteer to be servants if they are not able to provide for themselves. Sometimes the servant is captured from another nation after a war.
- A servant therefore is part of the household of his master – The Bible refers to a female servant as a maid; the same rule is applicable to both of them; with God, they are measured by equal standards
- He represents his master; the request of his master takes precedence over his. He identifies with the needs and interests of his master
- A true servant is also a faithful servant; obeys his master and cares for and serves his children.

God shows us the example of a loyal and reliable servant in the life of Abraham's eldest servant who was sent under oath to go get a wife for his master son from among his master's kindred – Genesis 24.

He went about it diligently and faithfully relying on God to help him to accomplish his master's request. At every step of the way he showed his dependence on God and his love and dedication to his master.

Peter declares that as God's servants – 1Peter 2: 17; we are to honor all men including those in authority, love the brethren, and fear God. Your attitude to God, other people shows whom you serve and whom you serve shows where you are; for a servant is a part of the family of the master he serves!

In God's dealings with us as His servants, remember He blesses us so that we can be a blessing to others, same way He saved us so that we can reach out to other people too, for the Gospel must be preached to all the nations before the end of the earth.

- God expects us to occupy till Jesus comes back again, because He is coming again the same way He went up to heaven, the first time He came, in the clouds. He will come at the sound of the trump of the archangel, with the host of heaven, for His bride the church.
- The disciples were to start from Jerusalem. God will judge us based the level of His grace and the extent of His revealed will to each and every one. Each one is individually accountable to God. Ignorance is no excuse with Him. Hence the need to study to show ourselves approved a workman who need not be ashamed – 2 Timothy 2: 15.
- We are to expand and establish the kingdom everywhere and at all times, starting from where we are to other areas far away from us.
- He is coming for only the prepared, and expectant. Are you? God gave each and every one of us different gifts which He expects us to use and profit with, by building the Body of Christ.

- God expects us to be first servants if we must attain the status of a leader – leadership is a call to service in God's kingdom. Unlike in the world where the leaders lord it over their subjects; with God, as leaders, we are called to minister to the necessities of others. He demonstrated to the first disciples by washing their feet. Are you ready to serve?

We must be will therefore to find out God's purpose for His people and like Solomon ask God for wisdom to be able to minister to God and His children, so that we can make our call and election sure.

God is calling us to live victoriously and be over comers. This entails investing what He has given us so that we can be profitable.

Prayer Points:

Dear LORD, please help me to be profitable to You in every area of my life

WEEK 45

JOHN THE BAPTIST – A True Servant

Bible Passages: John 1: 32-34; Mark 1:1-9; Luke 7: 28

John 1: 32-34
32 And John bare record, saying, I am saw the Spirit descending from heaven like a dove, and it abode upon him...

Jesus testified of John the Baptist ... *Among those that are born of women there is not a greater prophet than John the Baptist...* John the son of Elizabeth and Zechariah was the cousin of Jesus. He came with a mission, and pursued his destiny and call with zeal, vigor, and determination.

He was not swayed by public opinion, or the norm of the society. Consider some of his attributes: -
- He did not allow the fact that he was an only child and born by old parents to get him out of God's plan and purpose for his life. This involved a life of discipline and self denial.
- He presented the message of repentance to both great and small without allowing the position and power of Herod to dissuade him from speaking against what was wrong – sin is sin, no matter who commits it!

- He pointed the attention of the people to Jesus. This is what we are called to do as we preach the Gospel. God has commissioned us to preach the Gospel.
- He has not called us to preach our successes and achievements; neither has He commissioned us to emphasize our failures. Our messages must always point the attention of the people to the Messiah, the only one who can save and deliver. It is true that
- Jesus truly must increase while we decrease, for He it is that must be glorified, honored and manifested in the midst of His people – Paul stated that he preaches Christ only and He magnified. He was the one crucified and rose again is now seated at the right hand of God the Father. and glorified, not you!

Who do you preach? The more we point people to Christ, the more He manifests Himself in our lives. Everything we do must be turn to the attention of people to Jesus who is the Author and Finisher of our faith.

This then is then is a great lesson to learn from the life and ministry of John the Baptist.

Whose Report Will You Believe?

Bible Passages: Proverbs 15; Numbers 13-14

In dealing with the issues and challenges of our lives as we advance to the Promised Land (goals; objectives and visions) we are faced with dealing with the apparent situations and circumstances.

Sometimes these appear to be contrary to the promise God has given us. The questions you should consider are these:
- What is God's report of Himself concerning the issues at hand? What is your report? What are other people's report concerning the issues at hand?
- Whose report will you believe? What is your choice? What are you going to do with what your choice?

God expects us to take action; He judges our actions. Our response to what we see, hear or feel determines the extent to which we are able to take God by His word.

So if we are not progressing in the things He has told or shown us then we need to check our faith walk- Mark 9: 25. God empowers us to act and advance comes from trust that is faith in His word (report) – By faith
- Abraham moved to a city he never saw, because he heard God speak him to.
- Moses led the children of Israel out of Egypt, crossing the Red Sea on dry land while the Egyptians who attempted to do the same perished
- Joshua led the children of Israel into the Promised Land. Like the saints of old we are to subdue kingdoms by allowing the Holy Spirit to lead, guide and empower us to accomplish.

Prayer Points: To lift Jesus up in words and actions

WEEK 46

CAN THESE BONES LIVE?

📖 Bible Passages: Ezekiel 37; 1 Samuel 2; John 21

Ezekiel 37: 3-7
3 And he said unto me, Son of man, can these bones live? And I answered, O Lord GOD, thou knowest.
4 Again he said unto me, Prophesy upon these bones, and say unto...

them, O ye dry bones, hear the word of the LORD.ith God all things are possible; but we see through the Scriptures that God has always included human beings in His plans. Hence we see Him coming down from heaven to fellowship with

For instance He related with Adam and Eve in the Garden of Eden; walked with Enoch. He spared Noah and his family; started a new generation and made a covenant with him; called Abraham out his native country of the Chaldeans and brought him to Canaan.

He brought Jacob through Joseph to the land of Goshen in Egypt to spare them from famine and preserve the generation. God also related with Moses and used him to bring the children of Israel out of Egypt; and Joshua to take them to the Promised Land.

As these men and their wives and children related with God, He kept His promise of preserving humanity and making us to have rule over all that He created. Remember that even the animals bear the name they were given by Adam the first man.

God could have given these creatures their names, but He gave us a participatory role in the administration of the world! This thrilling! Ezekiel was right in his response to God – *Thou knoweth;* Same answer Peter gave Jesus when He asked if Peter loved Him. John 21:17 He knows all things.

- He knows the bones can live; the extent of our love for Him; and how much we desire Him
- He knows and can do all things; But He says, because He has given us authority, and that as He is in heaven so are we here on earth. Therefore:
- Whosoever sin we forgive is forgiven
- Whatsoever we bind on earth is bound in heaven
- If we say to this mountain to move it shall move – we can prevail over every hindrance along the path of progress.
- We can heal the sick, and cast out devils in the name of Jesus. Whatsoever we ask in the name of Jesus our Father grants us.

These however are possible to all that are redeemed by the blood of the Lamb; that is born again. Are you born again?

And we must abide in Him, so that we can be fruit. We are to operate in love, knowing that God is Love. Love endures forever. We are to rejoice more that our names are written in the Book of Life. Spiritual authority amounts to nothing to a lost soul

Some of these men and women have been allowed into our lives for specific assignments. Others are to be witnesses of the goodness of God in our lives. Seeing God's miracles in our lives would cause them to turn to God, so we should not be mindful of their attitude.

Rather we should look up to God, who can turn them where so ever He pleases. Sometimes we do not know why He allows some people or creatures into our lives. Eventually we find out that they have been purposed, prepared, and/or equipped to participate in our endeavors.

These persons or creatures under the orchestration of God by whom and for whom all things were made, work for our good no matter their intents might be – Romans 8: 28.

The sisters of Lazarus; sent for and trusted Jesus to do something even after he was dead and buried. Those who were around helped roll away the stone from the grave yard; and remove the grave clothes from him. Ultimately Jesus called him out of the grave and gave him life back.

With the Messiah in our lives though we were dead, we can live again, because He is the resurrection and the life. It does not matter how far rotten the body has gone.

We are to seek His face as we relate with others, so that we can be whom God wants us to be to them as well as allowing them to fulfill God's purpose for allowing us to meet with them. We can call on the behalf of others too, just like Mary and Martha called on the behalf of Lazarus and the prophet Ezekiel called on the behalf of the house of Israel

We have been given authority and responsibility to pray and call forth (to life), those that are relevant to the issues of our lives at every particular point in time. We pray that it will please God to give us grace to see Him in all those He has placed in out path.

Prayer Points:

That every deadness in me to come to life

WEEK 47

BEHOLD A VIRGIN SHALL BEAR A SON…

Bible Passages: Isaiah 7-9; 53; Luke 1; Acts 1; 1 Thessalonians 4

Revelation 19: 10, states that the testimony of Jesus is the spirit of prophecy. All through the Scriptures, we see God dealing with His people including us the redeemed of the LORD, by prophecy. Psalm 25; Proverbs 3: and Daniel 2; and Deuteronomy 29, shows that God DOES NOT OPERATE IN SECRECY!

From Psalm 91 we see that we can choose to abide in His secret place, where He makes His plans and purposes known to His servants the prophets.

Notice that Paul admonishes us to advance to being God's servants in Christ Jesus, not just His children! God reveals His secrets to His servants; this implies that if we desire to know His plans and purposes (His secret), we must dwell in His presence (His Secret Place – the place of prayer, worship and meditation on His Word)

Can you truly say you are God's servant?
Where so you dwell? Notice that all believers are called to this position, but each one must individually accept the responsibility in order to enjoy the privilege of being kept informed of God's plan – Read Revelation 1

When Jesus came the first time there was expectancy on the part of the Jews who were the custodians of the promise, but there was no evidence of preparedness.
- Paul states that God has prepared great things for those who love Him which are revealed to us by His Spirit. There is an expected end (a hope) that awaits us in Christ Jesus – Jeremiah 29: 11. Jesus will come again the same way He went to heaven the first time He came – in the clouds
- We must expect and be PREPARED for His return, by praying and watching; not being pushed to and fro with every wave of doctrine; not indulging in unprofitable ventures and diversionary activities. We are to work out our salvation with fear and trembling; though at the mercy of God our salvation requires our active participation.
- Christ who was raised from the dead, and is now alive, will come again for both the dead and the living IN HIM, so we have victory over death.

JESUS CHRIST – The Way to the Father

Bible Passages: Hebrews 4: 14-16;10; Exodus 25-27; John 1

Let us look into The Tabernacle, which was Israel's mobile worship center.

We want to focus on our relationship with God, through His Son Jesus Christ. Let us take a look at the various aspects of the Tabernacle –

The Furnishings; Coverings; and Courtyard, each symbolize some aspect of our life with God, in the realm of our spiritual lives. We must approach Him:
- The Sacrifice; Being Cleansed by the water and
- Entering the Holy Place in worship

For Israel, the Temple became the seat of spiritual life. Now we have church buildings as places to physically congregate, though the activities are aimed at reaching God as we also fellowship with one another according to His Word. The Tabernacle in its essence, pictures the relationship we believers have with God through His Son, Jesus the Christ, who is our High Priest.

Moses' Tabernacle served as the place where God met with the people, and symbolizes the perfect approach to God that we have been given through the blood of Christ, who "tabernacled" with us while on earth. Because of the perfect offering of Jesus Christ – an unblemished, perfectly acceptable sacrifice made once for all time – we have redemption and eternal life.

Hence, we can enter boldly the Holy of Holies, to fellowship with our Father and God – John 1: 14. We no longer need to go through a laborious process of the slaughter of animals to obtain blood for sprinkling, for Christ has offered Himself once and for all.

All we need do now is to appropriate this, by accepting Him as Lord and Savior The veil that covers the Holy of Holies was turn at the time of His crucifixion, so we now have direct access to the Father.

Prayer Point:

That my eyes may see the Way and the Truth

WEEK 48

NEVER THE LESS AT THY WORD...

📖 Bible Passages: 1 Samuel 15; Isaiah 1: 19; Matthew 26; Mark 14; Luke 5:1-11; 22: 42

1 Samuel 15: 22 *And Samuel said, Hath the LORD as great delight in burnt offerings and sacrifices, as in obeying the voice of the LORD? Behold, to obey is better than sacrifice, and to hearken than the fat of rams.*

The word NEVERTHELESS appears 32 times in the New Testament of the King James Version of the Bible. However we want to consider how Peter used it in response to the instruction he received from Jesus after he and his partners (James and John the sons of Zebedee), labored all night without success at the Sea of Galilee.

They allowed Jesus to use their boat to preach to the people; after which Jesus told them to launch out their nets for a drought. By all scientific knowledge the day time was not the right time to fish. However Peter and his colleagues did not know yet that they were in the company of the One who made the seas and the oceans. Day and night times; and to Him all creatures are subject.

> They were yet to know Him also as the rewarder of them that diligently seek Him. Subsequently also they learnt from Him that it is more blessed to give than to receive.

There is one thing that was needful and necessary for Simon Peter and His friends to know and that is; it is not our responsibility to know how God will give us the blessings of the deep which He promised.

He demands full and complete obedience from us just like He did to His and our Father.

At the Garden of Gethsemane He prayed also for God to remove the cup of death on the cross from Him; but quickly added ...*nevertheless not my will, but thin, be done* – Luke 22: 42.

God is the great provider and His provision is according to His riches in glory by Christ Jesus, which is infinite and limitless; not based on our human understanding. As a matter of fact whatever knowledge we have is what He reveals to us; some of which is recorded and gives us opportunity to acquire such knowledge.

Therefore in order to enjoy His promises and blessings, that is PROSPER, believers must to learn to and be willing to abide in the Word of God. Remember our God is a God of plan, purpose and order. We are expected to fall into His divine plan and order. The great lessons that we as believers must learn in order to be able to eat the fruit of the land including that of the deep like these disciples did in this encounter with the Great Provider are:

> There is reward for giving God out time, talent and resources; knowing that everything we have or may ever have come from Him anyway. Be expectant of His blessings.

- He is Lord over all and He can do all things, with Him nothing is impossible. He is not limited by Science, Geography or any human knowledge, law or understanding.

- How much of your time and resources are you willing to give God? God is the One who owns us, our resources and time; so when we give Him our time we are giving back what actually belongs to Him. We cannot out give Him!
- He can choose to transcend every universal law to effect or affect the desired changes; does not owe any man, but He rewards every good deed and judges every evil action and thought. There was reward for Peter and His partners for allowing Jesus to use their boat. We must have the right answers to these questions.
- How far can you go in your obedience of God's Word? He demands complete obedience; partial obedience is as good as disobedience; and He judges ALL disobedience. He sees the heart! We must respond to His command with simple, pure hearts – Esther 4: 16; Daniel 3: 16-18; Daniel Chapter Six
- How much acknowledgement can you give for your achievements and successes? Psalm 18: 16; 75: 6

Your answers to these questions show how far you can go with God and how prepared you are for His blessings – Proverbs 10: 22.

Prayer Points:

Dear LORD help me to give in love, in abundance or out my necessity.

WEEK 49

THREE WONDERFUL AND FOUR THINGS TO CONSIDER

Bible Passages: Job 26; Proverbs 30: 18-19

Proverbs 30: 18-19
*18 There be three things which are too wonderful for me, yea, four which I know not:
19 The way of an eagle in the air; the way of a serpent upon a rock; the way of a ship in the midst of the sea; and the way of a man with a maid.*

Just as the:
- Serpent must rely on instinct to know his destination as he passes on the rock.
- No one can trace his path to and from his shelter in the rocks; it finds its way back and forth!
- The eagle flies to and fro in the sky, looking for prey and takes food to its offspring in a secure place on the mountains, with no compass; it finds it way by relying on its God given instinct and sense of direction. There are no roads in the sky, yet the eagles never miss their destination
- The ship depends on a small rudder, a man made compass to navigate the seas. Without site of the land probably for days, yet it is safely taken across the seas by a few men and women who directs it to its destination. Yet no one can follow its direct path because there are no highways on the seas.
- We may never understand what pulls a man so strongly to a woman that he is always looking out to be with and please her.
- When a man is in love with a woman she cannot be wrong, whatsoever she does pleases him. Even so we may never understand that:

- The only Begotten Son of God will love us so much to leave His throne in heaven to come down to earth to face the shame of the cross, and shed His blood to reconcile us to the Father. He did not have to do it, but He chose to
- God chooses to give us freedom and liberty to participate in work of redemption by the privilege of preaching the Good News – the Gospel must be preached. With the great power the angels possess, they cannot preach the Gospel; neither can they repent once they miss it. His ways are past understanding, that is beyond us much as we can never be able to explain the activities of His creatures

The only explanation we have for all these is that it is GRACE; and His Providential Hand working in all of His creation for by grace are we saved, and by His mercies which are new every day, are we kept!

Three Things Go Well and Four Comely

Bible Passages: Proverbs 30: 29-31; Psalm 147: 1; Jeremiah 6: 2

Proverbs 30: 29-31
29 There be three things which go well, yea, four are comely in going.

The Psalmist says praise is comely! Agur the son of Jakeh writes in Proverbs 30 the four things which are comely. Jeremiah likens the daughter of Zion to a delicate and comely woman! – Jeremiah 6: 2.

The word comely means pleasing in appearance; proper or seemly behavior; or pleasing in appearance and attractive.

The Word of God through the Psalmist says that praise is comely; and four things are comely to behold; then God is calling our attention to these creatures. What are the features and characteristics that make them to be beautiful to behold? How is praise a proper?
- The lion does not turn from any one – it is not intimidated and is confident of its strength.
- The greyhound is fast and puts its speed and agility to use in the face of attack by predators. They are confident of their speed and agility.
- The he-goat is very persistent in its courtship of female goats and never takes no for an answer!

They are very domineering and fight to keep the female they choose to mate with. The king is sure of his power and authority, makes the laws and takes charge of the defense of his territory with boldness and confidence!

He is confident of the effectiveness of his authority and power. His subjects look up to him for direction and administration of justice. His word is the law! True praises are seen before God as coming from those who have confidence His grace and authority! Our praises must be offered confidently and with assurance that God is willing to accept them as sweet savor.

Prayer Point: That I may walk in my destiny

WEEK 50

GOD REWARDS DILIGENCE

Bible Passages: Proverbs 6: 6-11; 22: 29; 26: 12; 24: 332-34; 29: 20; Luke 15: 8; Hebrews 12: 15

Proverbs 22: 29 *Seest thou a man diligent in his business? he shall stand before kings; he shall not stand before mean men.*

Jesus in the parable of the woman who lost her ten silver coins, talked about how diligently she searched for them, because of the value of the coins. She was not ready to give up on them, so she sought diligently and persevered in her search until she found them.

Whether in spiritual matters or secular issues, the value we place on an object or a person determines how much effort we put into obtaining and keeping such. Note however that what operate in the physical are reflections of our spiritual lives. Spiritual advancement and success demand discipline and diligence.

First we must understand where we are and where we are heading, that is have visions and goals based on the Word of God and as revealed by the Holy Spirit – we know God's will for us by finding those things or areas where we are at our elementary – things we are at peace with doing.

Second we map out plans and strategies for achieving our goals and objectives – we compare our strategies with God's word to see if they are in tune and harmony with His recommended ways of doing things. He shows us how others in the Scriptures did and the outcome of such actions; sometime times how some other Christians are working things out and sometimes the craftiness of unbelievers.

1 Corinthians 3: 18-19. Jesus referred to the wisdom (shrewdness) of the children of this world in Luke 16: 8.

We are to be gentle but tough and determined. Having mapped out our plans and strategies, we are to abide in Christ and hold on to what God has given us. That is work diligently, for it is only then that we can stand before kings – achieve our goals. It is by diligently holding on that we do not draw back to perdition.

The flesh most times is not willing to go far, but we must allow the Holy Spirit to have rule over our lives. Thereby the flesh is subdued and put in its place of submission to the leading of the Holy Spirit.

All that diligently seek God finds Him; likewise all that diligently look to the appearing of His Son shall not be disappointed

It Is More Blessed To Give...

Bible Passages: Acts 20: 30-36; Luke 6: 1-38; John 3: 16; 1 John 4

Acts 20: 35
I have shewed you all things, how that so labouring ye ought to support the weak, and to remember the words of the Lord Jesus, how he said, It is more blessed to give than to receive.

One major aspect of God's relationship with man is giving. The key message of salvation is that because of God's love for humanity, He GAVE His only Begotten Son Jesus to die for us. John the beloved apostle state that God is love, and Jesus told that God is Spirit and we must worship (relate with Him) in spirit and truth.

It is only the regenerated spirit that can relate with God. We are regenerated by the gift of salvation when we repent and accept the atoning sacrifice of Jesus at the cross of Calvary and His resurrection.

So we are redeemed, because Jesus gave His life for us and we accepting that in return give ours to Him. It is only by walking with Him in His footsteps that we can truly stand as He expects us to.

For must acknowledge that in Christ Jesus who upholds all things by the word of His power, all things consist – Hebrews 1; The preacher in Ecclesiastes states that naked we came and as such we will live; since we brought nothing to the world.

The Psalmist says *my times are in thy hand* – Psalm 31:15; it follows therefore that whatever we have belongs to Him, and He gave it to us so that they can be used here on earth. We do not need the possessions, gifts and not even the anointing in heaven. So let us give out of the abundance that He gave us; and even out of necessity.

He blesses us so we can be a blessing to others; so let's not be like the rich fool whose first thought was to save for the future when he got a good harvest. In obedience to God's word, let us allow the future to take care of itself; for the God who beautifies the lilies; clothes the beasts of the field and provides for the birds of the air. His provision for these does not fail.

Prayer Points:

Ability to give liberally and consistently

WEEK 51

WALKING WITH GOD: ENOCH

 Bible Passages: Genesis 5; Jude

Genesis 5:22-24
22 And Enoch walked with God after he begat Methuselah three hundred years, and begat sons and daughters:
23 And all the days of Enoch were three hundred sixty and five years:...

The last prophet of the Jewish dispensation was John the Baptist. The book of Jude states that Enoch prophesied of the coming of the Lord "with ten thousands of his saints"; so we know that he was a prophet of the Lord. It is to be noted that only a few lines was dedicated to the life of this great man, with a glorious testimony that walking with and being in harmony with God is eternally rewarding.

- This Enoch was very unpopular; one of the few men against whom nothing is recorded in the Bible. The other Enoch built a city, was so famous, and went with the city he built; yet the influence of this man, who was gifted with the spirit of prophecy, and who walked with God, is still fresh on the world today.

- He saw the promises afar off, was persuaded of and embraced them; and by faith lived as one alive from the dead, yielding his members as instruments of righteousness unto God.
- People might think that Enoch had not the trials, and difficulties that saints of God have today.
- That would be a superficial view, he was surrounded by, and going through the midst of, a system of things that Satan has improved upon at the present moment. He lived in the midst of the world as Cain and his descendants.
- Enoch means dedicated, disciplined, well regulated, and was significant of his character. He was a dedicated man, his life was disciplined and his habits regulated by the guiding hand of God.
- The faith of Enoch drew God to walk with him; he maintained unbroken fellowship with God. A man in communion with God is one of heaven's greatest warriors! There is manifold blessing and reward for walking with God;

ARE YOU IN COMMUNION WITH GOD?

Ezra The Scribe – Israel's Revivalist

Bible Passages: Ezra; Nehemiah 8:; Romans 8; Joshua Chapter One

Romans 8: 34-39
34 Who is he that condemneth? It is Christ that died, yea rather, that is risen again, who is...

Three men bear this name in the Bible, but our focus is on the scribe and priest who led the returned captives in Jerusalem to make a new commitment to God's Law (orchestrated a revival).

He is a descendant of Aaron. He was trained in the knowledge of the Law, while living in captivity in Babylon – No condition should be able to separate us from the love of God and His law! Ezra gained favor during the reign of Artaxerxes, king of Persia.

He commissioned him to return to Jerusalem about 458 B.C., giving him a royal letter – Ezra 7: 11-16, granting him civil and religious authority, with the finances to furnish the Temple at Jerusalem.

This was already rebuilt by the returned exiles – Favor from God, who has the heart of the king in His hands, makes way, where there seems to be none. He was devoted to his God and the high standards of holiness and righteousness that He demanded from Israel.

When he arrived Jerusalem and n discovered that many of the Hebrew men and women had married foreign wives from surrounding nations contrary to God's instructions – Ezra 9: 1-15; 10: 1-17; he initiated a process of cleansing and purification.

It is not enough to find the fault, it must be rectified True leadership is not in the number of followers, but in the ability to, along with others follow after Christ's Footsteps, by seeking to know and obey God's Word.

God is looking for TRUE followers who will lead by example!

Prayer Points: For revival in our land

WEEK 52

THERE WAS NO ROOM FOR HIM AT THE INN!

Bible Passages: Luke 2; Matthew 7; John 15-17; Hebrews 12; 1 John 2; Revelation 3

Luke 2:7 -8
7 And she brought forth her firstborn son, and wrapped him in swaddling clothes, and laid him in a manger; because there was no room for them in the inn...

When Jesus was born, there was a decree from Caesar Augustus for a census in Israel, and Joseph being from Judea traveled from Nazareth where they lived to be counted in his native land of Bethlehem of Judea, with his wife Mary who was due to give birth to their first child!.

Whichever is the case, Jesus was born at the manger with some shepherds close by. We have established that God is a God of plan, purpose and order, so these occurrences were not coincidences:
- He was conceived in a borrowed womb, because neither the blood of Joseph nor that of his wife Mary mingled with that of Jesus!

- He was born in Bethlehem – The Bread of Life was born in the city of Bread. At the time of His birth Herod ordered the killing of all the children within the age of His birth and his awareness of it
- At the arrival of the King of kings the king of this world went on rampage.
- He was born in the manger – The Chief Shepherd was born amongst sheep and shepherds.
- However He did not know that His Kingdom was not of this world and that He came to die to save all that will receive Him as little children!
- No one can take His life from Him, but at the appointed time He laid it down for all that will receive and appropriate His sacrifice.
- There was no room for Him at the inn – the inn is a temporary place of abode – Christ is not looking for a temporary residence in our lives.
- The first people to be informed of His birth were shepherds – He chose to announce His arrival to those who by their calling understood His mission.

The wise men came looking for Him from the east because they saw a star – It is not a coincidence that wise men sought the Wisdom of God; knowing that the deep calls to the deep.

And today wise men still seek, not stuck to finding Him in the palace but He is in all places. For He told the disciples in Matthew 7: 7 *Ask, and it shall be given you; seek, and ye shall find; knock, and it shall be opened unto you:*

So we have assurance that whatever we seek, we find; but wisdom will cause us to seek the God who can give us all things! Whom do you seek? You choice will determine the category you belong to – foolish or wise.

The wise seeks Him.
- Likewise when He died, He was buried in a borrowed tomb. He knew He would not need the tomb forever, but that it was just for a brief stay. He did not need a personal one.
- Believers must understand and live in the realization that we are on earth for a very brief period. But that our real place of abode and residence is heaven. Jesus told us that we like Him are not of this world – John 15: 19; 17:14-17.
- The apostle John wrote in the general epistle not to love the world despite the fact that we live here -1 John 2; because we belong to God who is our Father.
- Paul also reminded us that we are ambassadors for Christ while here on earth – 2 Corinthians 5: 20. As ambassadors, we are definitely here temporarily. He rose from the dead and ascended into heaven for that is where
- He came from and where He and all that is redeemed belong. However He tells us that He will come again with the voice of the archangel and the trump of God to take us to where He is. However He is coming for the prepared and the expectant.

Are you expecting His soon return? Then you must be prepared! You might want to ask how I can prepare. The simple answers are: Believe in the Lord Jesus that He came to save you from sin and death. Receive Him as Lord and Savior

Prayer Points: Grace to respect those in leadership position.

IN CONCLUSION

As we conclude this weekly Devotional, let us pay attention to the fact that this is more of a guide to the Believer to help in cultivating the habit of studying and applying the Word of God to our everyday lives.

We see in the lives of the various example cited in the course of the year the importance of obeying the Word and instruction of the LORD, in our everyday lives. We can follow an instruction that we heard; and we can only hear from reading, and listening to the Word of God.

Moreover we can hear God's instructions through His servants. Examples are:
- God's instructions to Adam and Eve at the Garden of Eden, their disobedience and subsequent expulsion from the Garden – Genesis Chapters 1-3.
- Various instruction of God to, and His interactions with Abraham, Isaac and Jacob
- The deliverance of Israel from Egypt and subsequent establishment in the land of Canaan are results people listening to and following God's instructions

- Saul the first king of Israel knew about God's plan for his life when he went to Samuel to seek counsel concerning his father's lost asses – 1 Samuel Chapters Nine and Ten. Also in Saul's disobedience against the instruction of God concerning destroying the Amalekites in 1 Samuel 15.
- Jehoshaphat was given instruction on how to fight the war against the children of Moab, Ammon and the Ammonites – 2 Chronicles 20.

The list is endless for the Scriptures were written to help us learn from the various events, and activities therein. We must also learn to maintain a communication with God on a daily and consistent basis remember the Bible tells us to pray without ceasing.

Moreover we are to allow the Holy Spirit to have a free course in our lives, for any accomplishment we may ever have is through Him. Let us remember a portion of this Sunday School Song – **Pray every day, pray every day, pray every day**

> *Read your Bible, and pray every day*
> *Pray every day, Pray every day*
> *Read your Bible, and pray every day*
> *And you'll grow, grow, and grow*
>
> *Don't read your Bible and forget to pray*
> *Forget to pray, Forget to pray*
> *Don't read your Bible and forget to pray*
> *And you'll shrink, shrink and shrink?*

HOW TO BECOME A CHRISTIAN

You're not here by accident. Jesus loves you, and He wants you to have a personal relationship with Him.

- There is one thing that separates you from God; sin. People tend to divide themselves into groups – good and bad people. God says that every person that has ever lived is a sinner, and *any* sin separates us from God. That includes you and me. *For all have sinned and come short of the glory of God* – Romans 3:23

- According to man's rules, people should be punished or rewarded according to how good they are, and it might be hard for you to understand how Jesus could love you when other people don't. Jesus DOES love you more than you can ever imagine!

There' is nothing you can do to make Him stop loving you! Are you thinking that you should make things right in your life before you come to Jesus?

Many people feel that way, but that's not what God says! – Romans 5:8.

To come to God you have to get rid of your sin problem. But God says that you can't make yourself right with God by being a better person. God wants to save you JUST BECAUSE HE LOVES YOU! *He saved us, not because of righteous things we had done, but because of His mercy* – Titus 3:5

- For you to come to God, your sin must be paid for. God's gift to you is His son, Jesus, who paid the debt. *For the wages of sin is death, but the gift of God is eternal life in Jesus Christ our Lord* – Romans 6:23
- God's grace that allows you to come to Him - not your efforts to clean up your life, or work your way to Heaven. No one can earn it. It is a free gift. *For it is by grace you have been saved, through faith - and this not from yourselves, it is the gift of God* – Ephesians 2:8-9

- Jesus paid the price for your sin and mine by giving His life on Calvary's cross. God brought Jesus back from the dead and paved the way for us to have a personal relationship with Him through this same Jesus.
- All you have to do is to accept the gift that Jesus is has made available to you right now – Romans *10:9-10*
- God says that if you believe in His son, Jesus, you can live with Him forever, in glory. *For God so loved the world that He gave his one and only Son, that whoever believes in him shall not perish, but have eternal life.* – John 3:16 .Are you ready to accept the gift of eternal life that Jesus is offering you right now?
- If you have trusted Jesus as your Lord and Savior, we rejoice in what God has done in your life. If you sincerely desire to ask Jesus to come into your heart as your personal Lord and Savior, then talk to God from your heart:

    Here is a Suggested Prayer:

    Lord Jesus, I know that I am a sinner and I do not deserve eternal life. I believe You died and rose from the grave to purchase a place in Heaven for me. Jesus, come into my life, please forgive my sins and save me. I now place my trust in You alone for my salvation and I accept your free gift of eternal life.

REFERENCES

1. Master Christian Library - AGES SOFTWARE®, INC. • Version 8.7 © 2000-2003. Rio, WI USA
2. Nelsons Electronic Bible Reference Library©
Nelson Electronics, Inc 3911 Nelson House Road Ellicott City, MD. 21043-4838

3. Bible Explorer 4®

OTHER PUBLICATIONS BY MARGARET J MAKINDE

The Weapons of Our Warfare
(THE OVERCOMING ABILITY OF A BELIEVER)
ISBN: 978-1-4276-1833-7

In His Footsteps - First Edition
(A 52 Week Devotional)
ISBN 978-1-4276-1832-0

Overcoming Famine
(WHAT TO DO IN TIMES OF FAMINE)
ISBN 978-1-4276-1835-1

Fulfilling Destiny
(FULFILLING GOD'S PURPOSE)

ISBN 978-0-9840520-1-1

Praying Effectively
(THE ART OF PRAYING)
ISBN 978-0-9840-5200-4

In His Footsteps – 2
(A Fifty-Two Week Devotional)
!SBN 978-1463745981

Taming Our Environment
(Applying the Believer's Authority)
ISBN ISBN-13: 978-1463745721
ISBN-10: 1463745729

The Glad Tidings – Freely and internationally distributed

www.ingramcontent.com/pod-product-compliance
Lightning Source LLC
Chambersburg PA
CBHW071711090426
42738CB00009B/1737